D1825993

WING COMMANDER DIZZY ALLEN DFC

Fighter Station Supreme

RAF Tangmere

PANTHER
Granada Publishing

Panther Books
Granada Publishing Ltd
8 Grafton Street, London W1X 3LA

Published by Panther Books 1985

Copyright © Wing Commander H. R. Allen 1985

ISBN 0-586-06266-1

Printed and bound in Great Britain by
Collins, Glasgow

Set in Times

We took off into the lowering dusk and hung around the airfield at 2,000 feet. After a while he told us to land. He had lost track of the bandits and assumed they had returned to base. I sent my No 2 down but continued a lone patrol, but he kept screaming at me to land. I told him to go to the sick quarters and order a glass of cyanide, but eventually landed and rolled to the end of the runway.

The next thing I knew was tracer bullets crackling over my head accompanied by bloody great bangs. I leapt out, jumped in a ditch and unclipped my parachute. Then I sprinted to the dispersal where an airman was popping away with a Lewis machine gun. I was a better shot than he, so I took over the gun while he kept the ammunition belt straight, but I got in only a few bursts before the tail-enders were out of range. If I had been kept aloft for less than a minute, I would surely have shot down three of the Germans. I had sufficient vision to see their red-hot exhausts, but they hadn't a hope of seeing me. My vocabulary of invective and abuse would horrify the wife of any Billingsgate porter, and I gave the controller the full works. He applied to leave the fighter controller Branch and became a secretarial officer . . .

By the same author

Ten Fighter Boys
Air Warfare
The Legacy of Lord Trenchard
The Queen's Messenger
Battle for Britain
Who Won the Battle of Britain?
Buccaneer – Admiral Sir Henry Morgan
Spitfire Squadron
Fighter Squadron

DEDICATED TO: The Memory of RAF Tangmere, in the optimism that those who believe that Biggin Hill was the crack Station in Fighter Command think again.

THE LONG FAREWELL

Tangmere is closing down they say
They've dined the squadrons out, and soon
The wise face of the Hunter's moon
Will see them scattered far away.

The old pits where the fighters lay
Awaiting the marauding Hun,
Lie empty now, like ancient scars,
Weed-grown beneath the setting sun.

The squadrons climb against the sky,
Deep-etched upon the dying light,
The wind stirs softly, like a sigh,
For those who fly and those who fight.

This field, as famed as Agincourt,
Or Crecy, with their mailed hosts,
Where those who valued freedom fought,
Sleeps guarded by its valiant ghosts.

M. H. Hunt – *The Field*.

CHAPTER 1

The RAF Fighter Station at Tangmere could hardly be likened to a retreat where one could get away from it all, though that was eminently possible. Sudden death could claim you if your aircraft made a hole in the ground because of technical failure or German bullets. But that applied to most fighter stations based in southern England, so it can be left out of the argument. During my twenty years service with Fighter Command I served at every major station, a number of which looked like gypsy encampments. I can mention Biggin Hill, Kenley, West Malling, Hawkinge, Manston, Gravesend, Hornchurch, North Weald, Duxford, Coltishall – even Exeter to make the point. But there never was and never will be a station so attractive as Tangmere. The poetry of the name gives it away. I served for six tours of duty at Tangmere, and I'd like to meet anyone who knew it so intimately as I did.

It lies three miles to the east of Chichester, under the Goodwood Downs, which presented take off and landing hazards when using the short north/south runway. But the main runway stood firmly east to west with flat approaches, and the only hazard was the spire of Chichester cathedral which rears up to 270 feet. Many's the time I have all but removed the gargoyles in foul weather. For those with an aquatic bent, Bognor Regis is three miles away, but I side with Edward VII. On his death-bed he was informed that if he continued to live he would be sent to Bognor Regis to convalesce. He murmured, 'Bugger Bognor,' and turned up his toes. Punters have a merry old time, with the superb Goodwood race course, and the jumps at Fontwell. The Goodwood estate contains a gorgeous golf-course where pheasants strut across the fairways, and one can catch glimpses of the cathedral and the coast from on high. Yachting is another pastime, for Tangmere is well within range of Cowes and the rest.

Freddy Richmond is the present Duke of Richmond and Gordon, and a nicer man it would be difficult to meet. His grandfather went berserk when the Royal Flying Corps requisitioned part of the estate to construct an airfield. Schoolboy Freddy was delighted and spent his days on holiday from school cadging flips in clapped-out old biplanes. The *raison d'être* of the airfield was as a staging post to refuel aircraft en route to France. After the First War the RFC, now the RAF, decided to retain their lien on the airfield but didn't know what to do with it, which gave the old Duke apoplexy. To add insult to injury they forced the owner to sell them more land. At the time the potential enemy was France, which had by no means pared its air force to the bone as Lloyd George and his successors had done to the RAF. In the main, fighter stations were congregated around London, hastily improvised when the Germans began to bomb the Capital. It was therefore decided to convert Tangmere into a fully fledged fighter station for it was strategically beautifully situated against the (dubious) threat. But the throbbing heart of a station is reliant on the quality of the squadrons deployed, and by a freak of good fortune Nos 1 and 43 squadrons flew into Tangmere in 1926.

Many old hands, my contemporaries, gargle their beer in dispute, because they are naturally prejudiced in favour of the squadrons they served in. Thus No 56 squadron, for example, laid claim to being the crack fighter squadron because Captain Albert Ball, VC, DSO, MC, had served with it. They still have his uniform in a glass case to prove the point. But one individual, no matter how brilliant,

10

does not make a crack unit. No 1 squadron was the senior squadron in the RAF, and had seen plenty of action in France; so had No 43 squadron. But it was their coming together as sister squadrons, the terrible twins, that honed them into perfection. Inter-squadron rivalry played a large part in this transformation, and in short time they put Tangmere on the centre of the map. Between the wars they spawned fighter aces, and officers destined to reach high rank. Among others, two of their sergeant pilots, Frank Carey and Jim Hallowes, quickly became outright aces in World War II, were commissioned and went on to do further damage to the Luftwaffe. Jim Hallowes finished up commanding four fighter squadrons, only one less than I did.

The annual Hendon air pageants had something to do with this. This was a promotional exercise to popularize the RAF in the eyes of the electorate and thereby pressurize the politicians to increase the budget granted in the annual Air Estimates. Formations of large biplane bombers would attack Hendon airfield, the targets being wooden sheds. The faked screech of falling bombs would be relayed over Tannoy systems, and the sheds blown up by dynamite at the appropriate moment. Fighters would perform flight formation aerobatics, aircraft tied together with rope with bunting attached, and nice pilot judgement was necessary. A static display of aircraft types would be assembled on the ground, and I used to gaze in wonder at this useless array. As a young schoolboy I remember examining the Supermarine S6B, a float plane which won the Schneider Trophy in 1931, at a speed of more than 400 mph on the straight and level. I ducked under the protective rope and ran my hand along the fuselage before a sentry pulled me away by the ear.

The squadrons selected for flight aerobatics had to prove their ability against others before the Pageant, and in the course of time Nos 1 and 43 regularly defeated their opponents and performed over Hendon. No 43 became the most highly regarded fighter squadron in this sphere and gained fame in the process. There is no doubt that it became the crack fighter squadron in the RAF, and only hand-picked pilots were sent to serve on it. It was held in awe by pilots in the other RAF squadrons, no matter how secretly.

Circa 1938 both squadrons were re-equipped with Hurricanes. On the outbreak of war, No 1 was sent to France with three other squadrons to await its massacre by the Luftwaffe, and No 43 remained at Tangmere where it too had a rough time during the Battle of Britain. Tangmere was exposed to attack by the Luftwaffe. It was close by the shore and within easy range of German bombers based on the Pas de Calais, even Cherbourg. Its importance was easily recognized by the Germans and they promptly attacked it with their Stuka dive bombers accompanied by strafing fighters. Severe damage was inflicted on major installations, but the airfield remained more or less serviceable. One wing of the officers mess was badly damaged, and a nearby large house was requisitioned to make up the deficit. But like the Phoenix, Tangmere was destined to rise from the ashes and paint the skies with azure, white and red. Indeed, it was to become the most painful thorn of them all in the flesh of the Luftwaffe.

CHAPTER 2

It will help if I briefly outline my experiences in the first years of the war, before I reached Tangmere. My other books tell the story in more detail. I joined my first fighter squadron in April 1940, which gave me a little time to prepare for the holocaust. No 66 squadron was based at Duxford, near Cambridge, and was the second to be equipped with Spitfires, the supreme fighter, a thoroughbred whereas the Hurricane was a tough old hack. It was commanded by Rupert Leigh, a burly bloke with an almost incomprehensible sense of the ridiculous. He should never have joined the Air Force even though he rose to Air rank; he should have been the conductor of an orchestra. Music controlled his soul. Today I rate him as my best friend – we share so many memories no matter how grisly. In short time he decided that I should be his No 2, his wingman, and as he almost invariably led the squadron into action, I saw more action than most other pilots whether I liked it or not. Considering that we often flew five sorties a day against overwhelming odds, I confess that I often wished for the relative comfort of a cell in a monastery even as senior campanologist. But we had our moments, and although it is utterly exhausting flying to heights greater than Mount Everest in unpressurized aircraft several times a day, we were not always too tired to go out on the tiles for a booze-up. Pure oxygen was our lifeline but occasionally it was tainted which gave nasty side-effects. I once watched one of our pilots peel off and go into a vertical dive, followed him down and bawled at him over the R/T. He never recovered from anoxia and felt nothing as his Spitfire made a hole in the ground big as a bomb crater. God knows how his oxygen flow dried up, but it obviously did.

We gained combat experience intercepting lone recce bombers over the North Sea, and were redeployed to a couple of other stations in the backwaters. A couple of pilots were shot down by rear gunners, and several more just managed to escape death crash landing their combat damaged Spitfires. When the Luftwaffe put the heat on we were moved to the front line of 11 Group, and landed at

Kenley just after it had been severely bombed. Burned out petrol bowsers and wrecked Hurricanes were everywhere, also a number of unexploded bombs which made things fairly precarious. The squadron we relieved was shot to pieces and the pilots ran in panic for the available aircraft and flew to a quiet area. I was mildly disgusted, but a squadron depends on its leadership.

We didn't do too well on our first squadron scramble when we ran into a mighty big balbo. One pilot was killed, another severely burned, and four were wounded. A chunk of lead penetrated my flying boot but I didn't report it. I don't trust medicos. Medicos have the lien to ground you. I kept away from the doctors. The wound hurt like hell mainly due to the bruise in the calf as the red hot bullet penetrated the flesh, but I continued to fly on the operational roster. A couple of days later I was shot up again, and one of my ailerons refused to function, but I approached the runway at high speed and drove the wheels onto the ground before she could go into an incipient spin on the approach. You've got to be adaptable to survive. We stayed at Kenley for only a week and I hated the place. It was a regular RAF station and the attempt was made to continue the bullshit and bang-me-arse. Then we flew to Gravesend where we stayed for fifty-five days.

Gravesend was a pre-war airport used as a flying club and large enough to accommodate only one squadron. We were loners; we preferred to be on our own. Strategically it was superbly placed, within easy range of the Kent and Sussex coastlines. Together with Hornchurch across the river it acted as a portcullis to hostiles following the Thames to London. Depending on the tracking of the raids, Rupert could gain height to the north, wheel around on a reciprocal heading, and either meet the bandits at the same height, or chase them if they had turned for France.

14

Astonishing enough, German Intelligence didn't seem to be aware of existence of this important airfield. Certainly we were never bombed during the two hectic months I was there, yet the very forward bases at Manston, Lympe and Hawkinge were regularly attacked; the latter two were in range of the Wermacht's heavy artillery! We didn't lose half the squadron on one sortie as we had at Kenley, but a number of our pilots were picked off almost daily. Our 'A' Flight Commander, Ken Gillies, was shot down by rear gunners in October, and his body was washed out of the Thames Estuary three weeks later. The indestructible identity tag we all wore proved that the bloated corpse was the remains of Ken. This was a shock, especially to Rupert for Ken was his best friend, but he retained his poker face and pressed on regardless. Ken was an exceptional pilot and part of the hard core of the squadron, but he took a risk which didn't pay off. But pilots who joined the squadron at about the time I did and managed to survive were gaining in experience, and the squadron kept its head above water. Indeed, we received a congratulatory signal from on high for shooting down thirty Germans in a week without any fatalities. We certainly destroyed double the number of German aircraft than they did of ours.

Several pilots were severely burned, and one might as well go to hell as suffer that fate. The Spitfire was less prone to burning than the Hurricane, for its fuel tanks were outboard in the wings, and in due course self-sealing tanks were fitted. The same applied to the Hurricane, but some rock ape decided to insert a 30 gallon overload tank under the instrument panel by the pilot's feet. A couple of explosive German bullets penetrating that automatically meant that a pilot was immersed in an inferno, quite incapable of opening his cockpit canopy to bale out; in any case his parachute was probably on fire. A few managed

15

to achieve it, notably Richard Hilary, author of that classic *The Last Enemy*. If you want to know about severe burns, read it. He was kept alive on opium for months, and was stupidly allowed to return to flying duties. Apart from his physical injuries, the mental trauma this sensitive young man suffered was beyond human acceptance. He crashed into a Scottish mountain at night, and my instinct tells me he did this deliberately. Whoever allowed him to return to flying duties should have been shot.

But whatever our inner feelings, we kept a hilarious face on things. Rupert ensured that our morale was at high pitch, which was the job of a squadron commander. Our ground crews were superb and worked well before dawn into nightfall. I had my own Spitfire, or rather a number of Spitfires as I wrote off one after another, but the same squadron code letters were painted on the fuselages of the replacements – LZ-X. Each differed marginally but not significantly in its handling characteristics. If they became unserviceable, my engine fitter and airframe rigger would work through the night to get it serviceable. If the job was beyond their competence, NCO fitters would be called in to rectify the fault. When the guns were fired, canvas stuck on by dope which covered the gun ports would be blown into thin air, and a certain amount of speed was lost by the subsequent drag effects. On stalling the aircraft to land, howls like banshees would issue from the ports and alert the ever ready armourers who would insert full belts of ammunition in the guns. A fighter is merely a flying gun platform.

There were no squadron pilots to spare to travel to the factories and collect replacement Sptifires. Indeed, by October we were getting dangerously short of pilots, and most newcomers were being sent to front line units before their flying training was complete. We had to put them on the operational roster, but most of them lasted only a few sorties. A few who possessed the cat-like reflexes necessary in a fighter pilot survived, but the weight of leadership fell heavily on the shoulders of Rupert, his two flight commanders and a few experienced section leaders of whom I was one. The Air Transport Auxiliary was formed to fly in aircraft from the factories to the squadrons, and they gave me a pain in the neck. They were purely ferry pilots and could not *fly* aircraft in the true sense of the word. They could cope with the Hurricane, with its widely spaced undercarriage almost immune from damage through heavy landings, but few of them should ever have been allowed to touch the sensitive Spitfire. All too often they would touch down at Gravesend, which was by no means a long airfield, jam the brakes on with too much vigour, and cause the aircraft to rear onto its nose leaving the propeller embedded in the grass. Thus a brand-new Spitfire would be well and truly pranged, and would have to be sent back to the factory for extensive repairs.

CHAPTER 3

In October I was leading my flight chasing some fifty Messerschmitts scurrying for France. The Spitfire was only about 15 mph faster than the Mes and we were catching up only slowly. However, I kept out of sight of them and as we crossed the cliffs, I was at 800 yards range, but the maximum effective range of the Browning machine guns was 400 yards and tempting as it was I did not press the firing button. Well over the Channel my engine suddenly blew up and oil covered my windshield, so I turned for home. My oil pressure registered nil, and the glycol temperature was off the clock, so I switched off the magnetos before she caught on fire. I settled down in a glide, opened the canopy and stuck my head out for I couldn't see through the windshield. I estimated I would cross the coast over Folkestone at about 3,000 feet, which I did, whereupon British ack-ack opened fire on me. What the brown jobs thought they were doing shooting at an obvious Spitfire trailing black smoke I don't know. I landed at Hawkinge with my wheels down, whereas I should have belly-landed for Hawkinge was a very small airfield, and applied the brakes. They didn't work since the pneumatic cylinder which operated them had been holed. We hit the barbed wire at 60 mph and I clambered out pronto only to find that I had completely lost my memory.

They kept me in the sick-bay at Hawkinge for a week and then drove me back to Gravesend where Rupert took a look at me and told me to drive home for a week's sick-leave. I protested, but he said that flying and severe concussion didn't go together. In any case, I might forget who he was and shoot him down.

This incident had a hilarious epilogue. Years after the war ended various aero-archaeology societies began to sprout. A great number of British and German aircraft had dug themselves deep into British soil, some with pilots and aircrew aboard, some without. These volunteers decided to locate the various holes in the ground, by means of talking to villagers, farmers or their sons who had been around in 1940. They examined Air Ministry files, took note of combat reports and squadron archives, studied Luftwaffe reports – everything you could imagine. If there was a high probability of finding remains, some buried 30 feet under the soil in marshy land, they hired mechanical diggers in an attempt to excavate the remains. They were hugely successful, and brought to the surface

18

guns, pieces of fuselage and engines which they put on display in various small museums. Skeletons were brought to light and the coroners held inquests which seemed to me a waste of time. Items such as chronometers which could be made to work, cuff-links, wallets containing money and photographs were discovered, and also perfectly readable maps. Indestructible identity tags gave the name, rank and number of aircrews, but even without such information the searchers went through their records and identified them anyway.

I first made contact with them several years ago when they telephoned me announcing that they had just dug up a Messerschmitt which fell in someone's back garden near Maidstone. I had shot it down, they said, giving me the date and time. I told them not to be so bloody silly: how could they possibly identify me as the successful pilot? They invited me to look at my pilot's flying log book which happened to be handy, and to my astonishment my entry repeated what they had told me. From then on they have frequently sought my advice and I work quite closely with them. A few months ago they wrote and told me that Werner Mölders had shot me down when I crashed at Hawkinge in October 1940, and had claimed me as his 43rd victim.

Werner Mölders was one of Germany's top-scoring fighter pilots when he was killed, with claims to over 200 allied aircraft. He was obviously leading the gaggle of Messerschmitts my flight was ranging on, and the bead of my gun sight was directly aligned on him. Given less than a minute I would certainly have blown his head off. Thus if he had shot down 42 aircraft at that time, approximately 158 allied aeroplanes would have escaped his clutches thereafter. The obvious conclusion was that as I climbed on a reciprocal heading, he saw me pouring black smoke and decided to chalk me up as his 43rd victim. There is no question but that I was shot down by British ack ack, for when the engineers dismantled my engine they found pieces of shrapnel in the oil tank, some bearing British code markings. I wonder how many more of Molders' victories were deliberate lies. Mark you, he was not alone in this. I know all too many British aces who faked the books for reasons of honour and glory, but where is the honour when one is acting in a dishonourable manner. I wouldn't like to live with their consciences, but by now I expect they have brainwashed themselves into believing what were patent lies. No, I veered in the other direction and shot down a dozen more aircraft than I made claim to. My mind rests easy.

After my week of sick-leave I returned to the squadron to find that Rupert had been promoted and, to my great regret, posted elsewhere. His successor was Athol Forbes, the epitome of James Bond. As a matter of fact I had more operational experience than he did, but he had used his to better effect. Like Rupert he was ten years older than I, and he too had been a pre-war flying instructor. Young duchesses used to swoon and point to the bedroom when Athol attended a soirée, and he was quick to take advantage. He reinvigorated several of the dukedoms for when the old dukes were sticking pigs he was stuffing their wives. He was appointed a flight commander to the famous No 303 (Polish) squadron in August 1940. The Poles were based on Northolt and held in a training capacity, much to their chagrin, for a number of them had seen action in Central Europe and France. The AOC-in-C, Lord Dowding, totally lacked imagination and even when the hard pressed No 11 Group Commander, Sir Keith Park, declared the squadron fit for combat, Dowding disagreed.

So it was on one fine September day, Athol was leading them on an exercise sortie when they spotted a balbo of

Huns. There was jabber over the R/T and they vanished leaving him on his own. He had no recourse but to follow them and they decimated the balbo. After that they were certainly placed on the combat ready roster and the Luftwaffe suffered accordingly. The squadron produced the highest scoring pilot in the Battle of Britain, who was in fact a Czech. When Athol took command of No 66 squadron, on his tunic he sported the ribbons of the Polish VC, the Virtuti Militari, and the DFC and bar. Even so he had to find out how we managed our affairs. The Poles were a gang of undisciplined lunatics despite their prowess. There was room for only one such squadron in Fighter Command, but Athol soon learned the ropes.

By this time my friend Bobby Oxspring had been appointed to command 'A' Flight and he had been with the squadron longer than myself. In due course Athol had me promoted to 'B' Flight commander, and the three of us shared the lead if one or other took a day off to do some shopping in London, another was indisposed and so on. As the winter weather approached, the Luftwaffe tended to stay on the ground, but Athol and I thought we would keep them on their toes. We cooked up rhubarb sorties during which we would fly at sea level to France, climb to increase our visual horizon and search for military targets. Army convoys were ideal, but we could also do a lot of damage to steam locomotives, troop trains, barrack blocks and the rest. Ideally we wanted a cloud base of 300 feet so that we could nip into cloud if the flak became too lethal, and reasonable visibility.

We didn't ask for authorization from 11 Group for these operations because it would have been refused. If anyone wanted to know what we were up to, the standard reply was that we had been flying a weather recce over mid-Channel. One day the weather was suitable and Athol decided to strafe a barrack block behind Calais and any other opportunity target that came our way. He said he knew a prominent bistro in Calais which would provide him with an excellent pin-point en route to the target, and off we set. We bust a locomotive and strafed a military convoy; I also took a pot-shot at a staff car, but we didn't find the barracks.

'Strange,' he mused when we landed, 'I didn't see my bistro.'

'Not really, Sir,' I said. 'You made landfall over Boulogne!'

Of course, British Intelligence got down wind of German military installations being burned by strange aircraft, but enquiries failed to identify the culprits. However, 11 Group decided to make rhubarb standard operational procedure but with disastrous results. Athol and I planned our missions very carefully, and the weather had to be just right. The Staff had no idea of such subtle nuances, and in any case we were thinking of stopping our operations because the Germans had fortified their flak barrier no end. The Staff soon called off rhubarb because the casualty rate was running off the graph. It is all very well to chance your luck by the use of surprise, but you are a bloody fool to take risks when the element of surprise has vanished. Curiously enough, among other things, a fighter pilot has to have an effective brain, even though many of those I met didn't.

Air Controllers could be equally lacking in the upper storey. It was entirely due to their stupidity that my Spitfire and I were severely mauled by Messerschmitts in February 1941. I managed to land the damaged aircraft at Biggin Hill (where we had been redeployed from Gravesend).

They counted 43 bullet holes plus one made by a cannon shell in the fuselage, and eventually dispatched the battered Spitfire by road to Eastleigh in case any parts could be salvaged. They sent me to Guys Hospital which had been dispersed to Orpington down the road from Biggin. They removed some chunks of lead and left others, which took them four hours, and part of the time the surgeon had to work under X-ray conditions. Four days later I called on the Medical Superintendent with my arm in a sling and announced that I was discharging myself.

'You can't do that!' he bawled. 'I want you here for another month.'

'Don't you know there's a war on?' I replied.

'But you can't fly a Spitfire with one arm,' he protested.

'It's a piece of cake, Doc,' I informed him. 'I landed the bloody thing with one hand didn't I? Anyway, I've got a qualified nurse who accompanies me. Actually she's my mistress, but she's a trained nurse for all that. I'd be obliged if you would give me a medical pack and she can change the dressings.'

My 'nurse' was my batman, and the nearest he'd been to a hospital was when he attended an abattoir as an apprentice butcher. But I survived the agony.

CHAPTER 4

Shortly after all that they thought we needed a rest from operations and sent us west to Exeter, a fine city before the Germans flattened it. One evening the controller rang up and invited me to fly an airfield protection mission with my No 2, as a formation of German bombers was coasting in. I told him to scramble the whole of my flight and bring the other flight to immediate readiness, but he said he had the situation under control and a squadron of Hurricanes was on an interception course. I informed him that a

Junkers 88 was faster than a Hurricane and he should get his head examined pronto. We took off into the lowering dusk and hung around the airfield at 2,000 feet. After a while he told us to land. He had lost track of the bandits and assumed they had returned to base. I sent my No 2 down but continued a lone patrol, but he kept screaming at me to land. I told him to go to the sick quarters and order a glass of cyanide, but eventually landed and rolled to the end of the runway.

The next thing I knew was tracer bullets crackling over my head accompanied by bloody great bangs. I leapt out, jumped in a ditch and unclipped my parachute. Then I sprinted to the dispersal where an airman was popping away with a Lewis machine gun. I was a better shot than he, so I took over the gun while he kept the ammunition belt straight, but I got in only a few bursts before the tail-enders were out of range. If I had been kept aloft for less than a minute, I would surely have shot down three of the Germans. I had sufficent vision to see their red-hot exhausts, but they hadn't a hope of seeing me. My vocabulary of invective and abuse would horrify the wife of any Billingsgate porter, and I gave the controller the full works. He applied to leave the fighter controller Branch and become a secretarial officer. They did a lot of damage to the airfield.

Soon we were sent even further west to open up an airstrip at Perranporth, a few hundred yards from the towering cliffs. Spume from the relentless Atlantic covered the aircraft and our cars and began the process of corrosion. We were given Spitfires with an extra 30 gallon fuel tank bolted to the port wing, outboard, but they were not intended for use in operations, merely for ferry flights when they would be removed on arrival at operational stations. But the rock apes on the Staff took the view that they now had a force of long-range combat Spitfires, neglecting the fact that the extra tank considerably increased our vulnerability. Consequently we were continually ordered to fly to airfields in East Anglia, and rendezvous next day with formations of Blenheims which flew to the Dutch coast on anti-shipping strikes and the like. We were purely anti-fighter escorts and it was not our job to penetrate the flak zone, but the Blenheims did and suffered a 75 per cent attrition rate.

In April 1941, Athol was promoted and sent to the Staff, leaving me in command. I joined No 66 squadron in April 1940 as an Acting Pilot Officer under probation, which was the scum of the RAF, served under Rupert for six months, then under Athol for a further six months, and while still in my twenty-first year, became boss of the unit. It was quite logical in fact. I was the last of the old-timers, the rest had been killed or maimed or posted elsewhere, and I had a sight more operational experience under my belt than either Rupert or Athol when they assumed command. They had older and wiser heads, but I was a crafty devil when it came to tactics.

We had to tie the Spitfires down to avoid having them blown over the cliffs in the howling gales and minor hurricanes, and it was impossible to taxi in high winds without an airman sitting on the rear of the fuselage else the aircraft would have reared onto its nose. One day I began to take off when I spotted in my rear view mirror two airmen hanging on for grim death, I had forgotten all about them. I said it was a leg pull and they said it bloody well wasn't after they jumped off. They wandered back to the dispersal, but so strong was the wind I was airborne in a hundred yards from that point.

I had my first and only technical failure in a Spitfire, which says an awful lot for the design considering I flew thousands of hours on them. One of my oleo legs refused to lock down and I decided to land on one wheel. I landed with full opposite aileron and kept it up until the air failed to provide sufficient strength to maintain lift. The wing-tip dropped gently on the runway and she skidded on for a few yards. The fitters jacked up the wing, bashed the oleo leg down with a sledge hammer, and towed her back to the dispersal. Some bloody fool had obviously made a heavy landing previously and failed to report it. They fixed the oleo leg and put on a new wingtip. I gave her a flight test and she was perfectly serviceable.

Other things I recollect. I was scrambled with my No 2 to investigate aircraft tracking from east to west far south of Eddystone lighthouse; by guess or by God I identified three German bombers covered by six Messerschmitts, probably flying an anti-shipping recce. My No 2 was a raw sergeant pilot who I was training in operations, but this operation was too much for him and I told him to return to base. I gained height over them and one Me followed me up which gave me every advantage. A quick burst blew him out of the sky. I spotted another closing from behind, out-turned him and hit his engine. His propeller came to a halt and he headed towards the sea, destined to die of exposure in about two minutes in the cold tumultuous Atlantic. So was I, come to think of it, if they got a lucky shot in my coolant tank. A third had a go and burst into flames after a short burst. I scanned the skies but it was empty; the remainder had vanished into thin air. In any case I had used a lot of petrol and landed back with only a few gallons of fuel in reserve.

We were called on to escort formations of a hundred British Bombers to attack Brest in daylight, which merely indicated the poverty of intellect of the Air Staff. Lying in harbour were the German capital ships *Gneisenau*, *Scharnhorst* and *Prinz Eugen*. Bomber Command attacked Brest night after night, but little damage was done. To attack by day was a disastrous decision. At the time the

Command were totally unable to hit specific targets; indeed when attacks were made on cities most of the bombs fell on the surrounding ploughland. The Germans could obliterate Brest with smoke at the touch of a button, and the flak defences were the heaviest in the world. The raids would be made at 15,000 feet, giving the Germans plenty of warning to fly in reinforcing fighters, as the radars picked the bombers up far out to sea.

We had no intention of entering the flak zone since German fighters would be kept out of the area. Our job was to ward them off on the approach and exit; but I had precious fewer resources than were required. Several raids were made until the Air Staff eventually came to their senses, and called the operation off. On every attack at least half the bombers were shot down. On one occasion I counted thirty parachutes descending. Later, the ships made their Channel dash to the Baltic; one struck a mine but they arrived intact. My old friend Bobby Oxspring, back on operations with another squadron, was the first to sight them, but they wouldn't believe him which wasted precious time. So much for the might of Bomber Command which, in fact, did not sink a ship at sea with free-falling bombs during the whole of the war. Perhaps Japanese admirals should have been invited to take command of the force.

I knew I was due to be sent on a rest from operations, but I kept putting off the moment by fiddling the books. I had one more aim in mind, which was to strafe an important bomber base on the Brest Peninsula. The plan was based on our old rhubarb attacks, with the difference that I would have to navigate for two hundred miles over a featureless sea. The target was at the very extremity of our range, there was no room for error, and I did not intend to lose any pilots. We took off at dawn on a day when the winds were slack so I didn't have to lay off much drift on my compasses. We flew just above sea level and my chronometer would indicate when we were making landfall. I concentrated on my compasses and the air speed indicator. Landfall loomed up as planned and I saw a black and white lighthouse which proved I was on course. We hauled up to clear the red cliffs of Brest and continued on course at tree-top level. German observers fired red Very cartridges to warn other posts along the line, and no doubt field telephones were buzzing, alerting the flak gunners at the airfield, Lannion. By a stroke of luck I sighted the airfield two miles to port and continued on course for nearly a minute before breaking R/T silence.

I told the squadron I was making a steep upward turn to port, then making a dive to ground level as we ranged on the airfield. They were to open up into loose line abreast formation, select an aircraft as their target, and above all beware of mid-air collisions. Then I ordered Buster, i.e. break the emergency seals on the throttle, and we came into the attack vigorously accelerating. I aimed at a Junkers 88 which began to burn, and men working on it were hurled into the air. On the perimeter track beyond there was a petrol bowser which I fired on. It exploded and flying debris engulfed the wooden sheds beyond. I took a look at the scene behind and saw a number of burning aircraft with others flat on their bellies.

I ordered the squadron to reform and waggled my wings so they could identify me. I weaved like the devil as we maintained tree-top height to put the flak gunners off their aim. We throttled back to conserve fuel and returned to base at sea level.

In due course, the Intelligence Officer and I debriefed the pilots and totted it up that we had destroyed eight bombers, damaged another four and destroyed various technical installations. The reaction of the Staff at Group HQ was predictable. Those who had not indulged in balloon operations in the Boer War strongly recommended that I be awarded the DSO. The AOC, who was the most stupid buffer I ever met and didn't know the difference between a Spitfire and a Hurricane, wanted to court-martial me. He reasoned that I had made an unauthorised attack, which was strictly against the rules, and I had unnecessarily endangered HM's aircraft! He was laughed out of court, but I didn't get a DSO.

A few weeks later, prisoner of war reports gave the information that we had destroyed twelve bombers. We suffered no losses. There's got to be a word for it. Try Surprise or perhaps Audacity.

CHAPTER 5

In April 1942 I was posted from command of No 66 squadron 'on rest from operational duties.' I don't know, but I believe it was a unique record to have remained with a fighter squadron for two years at that time. I had arrived with very little between my ears, but now I was an experienced fighter leader knowing almost every trick in the book. It was an education that could never have been bought, and it included man management, business efficiency, time and motion study, the ability to sum up a man at a glance, how to be rude to senior officers and get away with it, the quality of leadership which comes in many forms, and the knowledge that when a bullet penetrates your bum it is still red-hot. It had by no means proved I was a survivor, but I had survived. My successors were no survivors. The first lasted a fortnight. His successor lasted only two days before a rookie pilot collided with him in mid-air. That had happened to me, but I survived.

I asked to be given another flying appointment and

drove home on leave. The little twirps in the Personnel department think they are all powerful, and if you ask for a particular job they bend every effort to send you where you have no wish to go. They might have sent me to command a barrage balloon unit but, however reluctantly, I was appointed to command a non-operational squadron in Fighter Command with a special duties role. It had twelve different types of aircraft which I had never flown, and it was an enjoyable experience taming each type and thereby increasing my knowledge of airmanship. But then boredom set in and I volunteered to be seconded to the British Army, in the form of Air Adviser to the newly formed First Airborne Division. It was under command of Major-General Boy Browning who had served in the Grenadier Guards; he was a martinet and I wasn't over-impressed with his intellectual ability. Its two Brigades were the 1st Paratroops and the Air Landing Brigade which was training to carry troops and battlefield equipment when larger gliders were procured. The Air Landing commander was Brigadier Hoppie Hopkins and his Chief of Staff Colonel Pip Hicks. Pip was the epitome of a fighting soldier, even though he was 48 when I met him, and had been awarded the DSO in the First War. I took the view that he would be given the VC or die in the attempt, but as it was he gained a bar to his DSO at Arnhem where he held command for several days when General Urquhart was cut off from his command post. We struck up a strong friendship which endured until his death after the war.

My first piece of advice to Hoppie was to burn his bloody gliders and concentrate on parachuting. He had a good brain: he raised his eyebrows and asked me why. Hadn't German gliders virtually seized Crete single-handed, he enquired? True, but they lost their whole force in the process, and Crete was an unusual situation.

There were no Cretes in Germany. Gliders and their tug aircraft were far too vulnerable for reality. He intended to reduce that factor by making night landings, he informed me. I warned him that with no ground markers he could never produce sufficient concentration of force. I didn't manage to change the policy, of course, but my doubts were borne out as the war wore on. I made scores of friends with the Division, and they were particularly pleased when I got hold of a red beret and had a RAF cap badge sewn on. Strictly against the RAF dress regulations, of course, but my view is that regulations are there to be broken.

I stayed with them for six months and then asked Boy Browning to use his influence and get me sent to a fighter squadron, which he did. But alas the Personnel people made a balls of things. The present incumbent had been promoted Wing Commander and should have been sent to a post appropriate to his rank, but he pleaded that he had not much time on operations and could he be allowed to stay with the squadron. They swallowed this garbage and appointed me supernumerary to the unit, which meant that I had to fly under command of an apprentice. I should have refused and kicked up a row, but I had a feeling that he would be shot down soon when I would automatically assume command. I didn't trust his leadership nor his tactical nous, and used my own methods which didn't endear me to him.

There was a security clamp down in August prior to the ill-fated Dieppe raid, and what the planners thought they would achieve God might know but I don't. What they did achieve was to land 8,000 troops, mainly Canadians, who did nothing in particular. Only 2,000 returned to England. Our sector station and its satellite airfields confined all personnel to camp for a week ahead of the raid, and all public communications such as telephones and telegrams were cut off.

Airfields in 11 Group were reinforced by squadrons from the quiet areas, and thousands of fighter sorties were flown to cover the troops and naval escorts. The squadron I was attached to flew five sorties with no success, although there were hundreds of possible targets as the Luftwaffe reacted in force. The tactics adopted were wholly defensive, when the need for offence was obvious. I was utterly dismayed, indeed contemptuous. However, as dusk descended a section of Spitfires was retained at immediate readiness in case the Luftwaffe made retaliatory attacks. We were scrambled into broken cloud and I dimly perceived a bomber hopping in and out of cloud. I gave no warning but bust my throttle seals, and headed in that direction. A Heinkel 111 slipped out of cloud in close range, and I gave it a long burst with my cannon. It vanished into cloud but I saw a red glow just ahead and above. It had clearly exploded. I pin-pointed my position which was six miles south of Portsmouth and returned to base.

I filed a combat report, the Intelligence checked for any other claims made at the same time, and awarded me one He-111 destroyed. A couple of hours later the IO saw me and sheepishly informed me that my claim had been denied. British ack-ack had also claimed a bomber destroyed in that area at the time and they had been credited with it.

'Of course they might have shot down a bomber in the area,' I pointed out. 'But mine was six miles south of Portsmouth, far out of their range. In any case, the target was cloud-hopping and they hadn't got a hope of seeing it. What guns did they use? Big Berthas?'

'Sorry,' he said, and sidled off. I went to see the Sector Commander.

'I'm surprised you didn't come and see me before,' he said. 'Anyway, I'll try and fix you up with a change of air.'

It was not a happy sojourn, but the good thing was that it acquainted me with Tangmere for the first time. The squadron was based at a primitive airfield called Merston, half a dozen miles south of Tangmere itself which was the Sector station. We had our rooms in a requisitioned mansion near Tangmere, but I had time to get the feel for the Master station, which appealed to me very much. I also explored the surrounding countryside and the city of Chichester. However, after I had asked to leave I was sent to command a fighter airfield on which two Spitfire squadrons were based, which wasn't very difficult. This didn't last long, for a crisis loomed in Fighter Command.

During the Dieppe raid our pilots took hundreds of yards of cine film, exposed by cameras when the guns were fired. These were sent to the Air Ministry for scientific analysis and compared with the pilots' combat reports. The scientists quickly came to the astonishing conclusion that 80 per cent of our modern fighter pilots couldn't shoot straight. They would report, for example, that they opened fire at 400 yards, but their films proved that the range was 1,000 yards, meaning that all their ammunition was wasted. It was therefore decided to form a gunnery school, and a dozen experienced fighter leaders, including myself, joined it. It was under command of the redoubtable Sailor Malan, the most effective squadron commander in the Battle of Britain, and he could certainly shoot straight – and so could I.

We spent two months polishing up the techniques, firing at high speed drogues, indulging in dogfights in pairs, using cameras not cannon. Every day there would be sessions in clay pigeon shooting, and once a week we would go to the neighbouring farms and shoot driven game; a right and left at fast flying partridges is always good shooting. Much time was spent in lecture rooms running through the theory of fixed gun marksmanship, range estimation, angle off, the deflection or lead required when aiming from the quarter or the beam, line of sight – aim above a climbing target and below one on the dive, the effect of bullet drop and so on. A new type of gun-sight based on gyros was being developed, and we used prototypes to get the hang of things, which was quite difficult.

We refreshed our aircraft recognition by flashing through projectors photographs of British and German aircraft. These were on the screen for only a mini-second, but the mind's eye recorded the details for a few seconds more. But most important, we learned to assess with considerable accuracy combat and practice cine films. At first, we required measuring equipment to achieve this, but soon we could spot all the sighting errors simply by running the films through.

CHAPTER 6

It was never the policy to put all wing leaders and squadron commanders through the Fighter Gunnery School, which when computed would have been vastly expensive, and would have provoked a serious shortage of some of the most experienced pilots in the front line. No, the aim was to procure a nucleus of specialist gunnery officers, base them at the sectors, and let them spread the doctrine. Needless to say not every member of my course graduated with sufficiently high marks to be made a gunnery specialist – not many more than 60 per cent achieved that. Those who were successful were sent to various sector stations, and I was lucky enough to bag Tangmere, probably the largest of them all. Its major satellite was Ford, near Arundel, which had been an important Fleet Air Arm station and had concrete runways, hangars and the rest. A couple of miles towards the Goodwood Downs was Westhampnett where I established my office and my cine projection room; this was a grass airfield containing two squadrons. Then there was Merston on the way to Selsey Bill. I had more or less a roving commission.

The Sector Commander had received his terms of reference without any ifs or buts. I was to be given carte blanche for the purpose of greatly improving the standard of marksmanship; I was to be given full co-operation from the flying leaders; and I was to report directly to him as to progress or lack of it. If I wanted to stand a squadron down for operations for a day, then that would be done and other arrangements made to fill the gap. If I wanted to fly on operations with any squadron that would be arranged. This suited me very well as there were several different aircraft types in the various squadrons, each with its own role, which would allow me to cover the gamut of operations; squadron commanders, on the other hand, were limited to operations appropriate to their aircraft.

My first difficulty was to persuade the flying leaders that their pilots – often they themselves! – couldn't shoot straight. However, I had a supply of high speed drogues which could be towed by Spitfires at 300 mph, and each Spitfire also carried a cine-camera. I laid down a standard operating procedure for each squadron, had them roneoed and distributed. On days when they were detailed for gunnery training, flight commanders were to arrange for tug aircraft and attacking aircraft to take off at regular intervals to overfly the nearby gunnery range. This was a sector from the coast several miles out to sea declared a danger area for naval and merchant shipping when in use. The flying rosters would ensure that the range was fully utilized during the hours of daylight, and I would signal the Admiralty when it was opened and when we shut up shop for the day. When the mix of cannon and machine guns was fired, the cine-camera would also operate. Shell and bullets were dipped in different coloured paint per aircraft, so unless it was shot to ribbons, one drogue could accept up to three attacks before the tug pilot jettisoned the drogue on the airfield.

Careful records were kept of the colour of paint used by each pilot, and it was a simple matter to identify which pilot, if any, had hit the drogue. No pilot was to angle his attack less than twenty-five degrees from the drogue in case he erred too far and shot down the tug. Tracer ammunition was used and the tug pilot could easily take note if the angle of attack was dangerously fine, in which case he could order the pilot to return to base where I could check the facts. Concurrent with this, pairs of aircraft would also be detailed to fly inland, and one, then the other, would fly a long course straight and level while his colleague attacked him from all angles with his cine-camera, and on their way back they would mix it in a dogfight taking snap shots as in combat conditions. The facts began to dawn on flying leaders when it was apparent that very few pilots managed to put a hole in a drogue. My team of technicians would splice all the films together, inserting the name of each pilot on both firing and mere cine attacks.

At dusk, I would run the films through giving a commentary as to aiming errors and how to put them right. Some pilots wondered how I could be so glib in assessments, but I dealt with that by stopping the film and measuring the inaccuracies with instruments. That convinced them that I knew what I was talking about. I laid hands on some pornographic films, which made them look forward to the next gunnery session; and I promised to project two if their marksmanship improved. I requested that the squadron commanders appoint officers and deputies as squadron Gunnery Officers, and gave them special tuition so they could take part of the workload off my hands. I also told the wing and squadron leaders that as their films were spliced into the final reel, they had better come and have personal tuition. It wouldn't be good for morale if the pilots noted that their leaders couldn't shoot straight. This phase was like getting up steam in a locomotive, and it gathered momentum when I released the brakes.

Realization dawned that the average pilot never got within range of an enemy aircraft, but when he did so it was imperative not to lose the opportunity to destroy it. The importance of marksmanship was drilled into their heads.

On the sweeps over France, when guns were fired in anger, my photographic technicians would develop the combat films and copies would be sent together with the relevant combat reports to the Air Ministry via Intelligence sources. But in some extraordinary manner, no attempt was made to correlate the reports with the films. In other words, the assessment of whether German aircraft had been destroyed, probably damaged, or probably destroyed, was left entirely to the squadron IOs. If one or more pilots witnessed another pilot manoeuvring and confirmed that his victim exploded, all well and good. But on numerous occasions, pilots would report that they had shot down German aircraft with no witnesses save for the eye of the camera. I used to project these films before handing them to the squadrons, and make notes which I compared with the combat reports. It was not my business to accept or reject claims although I was in the best position to do so, I merely kept my mouth shut, but it was evident that 40 per cent of claims made were grossly exaggerated.

In subtle ways I dropped the hint to the squadron

commanders that they had better keep an eye on certain pilots who were over-enthusiastic in claiming victories, but that had little effect. When things got really beyond the pale I had to use tougher methods. I ran through a wing leader's combat film; he had claimed a Focke-Wulf 190 destroyed which was a falsification. I invited him to my workshop, ran the film through, and gave a running commentary.

'You opened fire at 1,200 yards and stopped firing at 900 yards,' I informed him.

'Yes. I used up all my cannon shell in one burst,' he said. 'The target burst into flame just before I ceased firing.'

'The maximum effective range of our cannon,' I pointed out, 'is 600 yards. With a great deal of luck a stray shell might cause mortal damage at 700 yards, but no more than that.'

'Are you suggesting that I'm fiddling the books?' he enquired heatedly.

'Oh no! Old Fritz might always have stamped out his cigar and caused petrol fumes in the cockpit to explode. But sure as eggs, you didn't shoot down that bloody FW-190.'

'What are you going to do about it?' he muttered.

'Nothing,' I replied. 'That's not my job. But better watch your step.'

In 1943/44 outrageous claims were being granted. Wing leaders such as this one seldom returned without making victory claims, and for every two such claims they were awarded decorations. Some of them were so weighted down with gongs that they could scarcely get out of their chairs. View all our war aces with grave suspicion. I can tell you those who had the necessary integrity not to indulge in the grimy search for honours.

CHAPTER 7

Within a few months the training machine was rolling of its own volition. All I had to do was to ensure that squadrons were stood down from operations when their turn came, and keep a general supervisory eye on things. Squadrons would assess the performance of individual pilots, for they had their own gunnery officers, and the squadron and flight commanders were now capable of assessing cine-films. This gave me time to fly more and more frequently on operations. The mix of fighters on the Sector and satellite airfields was interesting. At Ford there was a couple of Spitfire squadrons, and one equipped with American-built Havoc night fighters. The radar operators aboard the Havocs would be guided by ground control to five miles from the target when their own airborne radars (AI) could 'see' the target and they would guide the pilot to it. The best technique was to underfly the target, making use of the flames from the exhausts at close range, positively assess that it was German, reduce throttle to fall back into easy firing range and open fire. The Havoc was not much use in this role; it was only when the Mosquito was converted to night fighting that a drastic improvement came about. The Luftwaffe's night fighting ability, together with its sophisticated flak, was ferociously formidable at an early stage. *Eight thousand aircraft of Bomber Command* were shot down, and a great quantity were damaged during the course of the war. More aircrew were killed than all the British officers who lost their lives in World War I.

After the Battle of Britain and the night blitz on the UK, the heavy aircraft of the Luftwaffe began to be withdrawn and redeployed to attack Russia. An Air Fleet had already been moved to support Rommel in North Africa and to attack Malta. Coastal air defences had to protect the whole of Western Europe from Norway to Bordeaux. As the attacks on metropolitan Germany by Bomber Command increased dramatically, German day fighters had to be withdrawn to the heart of Germany to assist the night fighter force. These had to be greatly reinforced when US heavy bombers made daylight attacks on precision, bottle-neck targets which eventually brought German war production to a halt.

In 1941, British fighters swept French and Belgian coastal air space using multi-wing formations. German pilots could either respond or not as they pleased. They were pleased when the weather and tactical conditions were favourable, which also allowed them to assess the quality of their improved marques of Messerschmitts and the new Focke-Wulf 190. In 1941, Fighter Command lost far more fighters than the Luftwaffe, including Douglas Bader who was shot down by a German NCO pilot. This pricked Douglas's sense of pride having been defeated by a NCO, and his account of it all was that a Messerschmitt collided with him over France. The German NCO now runs a bar in Sydney, and being a Bavarian he can drink any of his customers under the table in a quarter of an hour. The Spitfire Mk II gave way to the Mk V which carried two 20 mm cannon and four machine guns, together with a souped-up Merlin. The FW-190 proved too manoeuvrable and it was necessary to modify the Spitfire again. The wing-tips were removed, which gave it a much faster aileron response, and 'the blower was cropped', which means that the engine supercharger was able to force several pounds more boost through the fuel system, thus improving its speed.

This was still not good enough against German fighters,

and the Mk IXA came along. This had a two-stage supercharger and on the climb, at about 20,000 feet, the pilot would flick on the second blower which increased the boost considerably in thin air. Then followed the Mk IXB in which the second blower came in automatically at around 20,000 feet. When the second stage blower came into action the pilot received a definite thump in the back as the aircraft began to accelerate. The blower on the Mk IXB was barometrically controlled, and this marque had the edge on conventional German fighters to the end of the war. There was further development potential even yet in the superlative Spitfire. As I will recount, I commanded a squadron of Mk XXIs which would have massacred the Mk IXB, but the war was coming to an end and there was no opportunity of proving the aircraft in combat. Specialist Spitfires were responsible for photo-reconaissance missions during the war. They carried no armament, merely cameras, and there were other modifications. Their all-up weight was considerably lessened, and they were painted blue to meld with the azure skies at great height. They flew so fast and so high that it was virtually impossible for German air defences to be alerted. In due course Mosquitoes, the most ubiquitous aircraft of the war, were also used in this role and they had a far greater radius of action than the Spitfire.

There was also the Mk XII with a four bladed propeller – the Mk XXI had six blades! These were short of altitude, but at medium height they could outpace any other British or German fighter. The Mk XIV was more powerful and even faster, but it too was constrained to medium height. The odd man out was the Typhoon, which looked not unlike an enlarged Hurricane. It had a massive 2,000 hp Napier Sabre engine which was nothing like as reliable as the Rolls-Royce Merlin, and it was of very strong construction. It lacked manoeuvrability and was hardly a fighter in the true sense of the word, but it found its forte when rocket batteries were slung under the wings in an anti-tank role. One rocket had the destructive power of a 3 inch shell, but they were difficult to aim accurately; it was even more difficult to penetrate the flak poured up by German tank columns, hence a great number of pilots were killed.

The Typhoon squadron based at Tangmere, No 486 was under the command of Desmond Scott. It was an all New Zealand outfit, as was No 485 run by Stan Grant at Westhampnett. Per capita in my estimation New Zealanders were the best fighter pilots of the war, but this really applied to those who joined Fighter Command before the war. Des was a tall big man, certainly one to be reckoned with. It wasn't difficult to get the gist of his instructions. He would say to his pilots before a mission: 'Now I've told you what to do and if you don't do it my way, I'll break your fucking knuckles.' I flew with all the squadrons in their different aircraft, and I had to remember what type I was flying as I taxied out. One day Des was ordered to attack shipping in Cherbourg harbour and he asked me to come along for the ride. I blanched at the prospect, which was so typical of the asininity of the rock apes at HQFC. 20 mm cannon cannot sink steel ships; the harbour would be heavily defended by ground and ship based flak; and the cost of one Typhoon and its pilot would exceed that of French and German ships damaged. But off we went.

Twelve Typhoons swept across the Channel at over 400 mph and at sea level. Cherbourg was crammed with shipping, including E boats and a destroyer or two, but in the main they were fishing smacks. Des ordered the squadron into sections echelon port, pulled up in a tight starboard turn, and aircraft attacked individually as briefed. I would not have done this, I would have attacked in section strength to confuse the gunners. Ship-born and ground flak whistled past my head as I dived, so I continued my dive to sea level, found a flak ship pouring fire, and silenced all its gun batteries. The squadron flew back to Tangmere in sedate fashion only to find one pilot who had returned prematurely. He was shaking like an aspen leaf and was as white as a virgin's wedding dress. As he dived to attack, flak had exploded under his tail fin and turned him on his back. He managed to regain control and scarpered back to base. Otherwise there were no casualties, by the grace of God. That evening Des ran the combat films through, making his own assessments as to marksmanship which he was entitled to do since I had taught him how. He stopped the film when my name appeared.

'Now we'll see how the fucking Sector Gunnery Officer did,' he said in menacing tone. 'And we'll watch it in slow motion.'

My ranging fire hit the sea ahead of the target, and then the flak stopped and men were thrown into the air. It was particularly noticeable that the flak guns were hit, although shell scattered all over the place, penetrating the wheel-house and so on.

'Not bad,' Des grumbled. 'But you opened fire out of range.'

I duly took him to one side.

'Look, you antipodean ape,' I said. 'With targets such as those, you must open fire out of range to keep the gunners' heads down. If you don't know that I'll have to give you special lessons in tactics.'

'Yeah. I suppose you've got a point.'

'Of course I've got a point. I was playing this game before you learned to fucking well fly. Come along to the Mess and I'll buy you a drink. Your boys did well to get out of that mess intact.'

The pure fighter side took on more significance when

43

the Americans agreed to use their light bombers to attack German airfields and similar targets within the coastal belts of France and the Low Countries. This forced the hard-pressed Luftwaffe to scramble their fighters in defence, but the Allies had the tactical advantages, and could mass overwhelming numbers. On their side, German pilots who baled out could return to their units, but Allied aircrew were made POWs. Fighter Command could climb wings to extreme altitudes, put up others as medium cover, and detail others to accompany the bomber formations as close escorts. I flew in different marques of Spitfires on these 'Circus' operations, sometimes as high cover, sometimes as close escort. Among other things, this gave me the opportunity of comparing the effectiveness of the various flying leaders.

I remember a formation of Maurauders bombing the airfield at Abbeville with extraordinary precision. No bombs dropped outside the boundary of the airfield, and as they exploded almost simultaneously there was a positive earthquake. I literally saw the earth ripple over a wide area. But the Germans were past masters at the art of immediate repairs and improvisation, and I am prepared to bet that Abbeville was serviceable enough for operations by dawn the next day. Bomber Harris and his Staff ordered Hamburg to be burned to the ground in July – August 1943. But by December, Hamburg's war production was greater than before the bombing. Bomber Command never learned, although the Americans did, that targets of all sorts need constant rebombing to keep them out of action.

CHAPTER 8

Squadrons were constantly rotated in and out of the Tangmere sector for various reasons, one being the need to rest units that have seen sufficient action. I would concentrate my efforts on the new boys to bring them up to the mark. Once a week I would go and see the Sector Commander and give him a situation report on the battleworthiness of the squadrons, and in some cases squadron and flight commanders of a poor rating squadron would be gently removed and replaced. One day he told me that a squadron of Americans would be arriving and that I was to give priority to training them in British techniques, such as air traffic, radar control and tactics. He said I had better treat them like eggs, especially since the squadron in question was en route from Texas and were bound to believe that the sun shone out of their arses. They duly arrived in their P-47s, the Thunderbolt, a big fat flying beer barrel with a radial engine. It had an enormous four bladed propeller, and carried four quick firing 0.5 inch Colt machine-guns, which were more like cannon than machine-guns and had double the effective range of our Brownings. A most important factor as things turned out was that the Thunderbolt carried very considerably more ammunition than any British fighter ever did. They had the range to fly to Aachen and back, whereas the Spitfire couldn't get as far as Paris.

They flew in their spares and ground equipment in transport aircraft and a gang of our airmen helped the ground crews to sort themselves out. The Sector Commander and I greeted the pilots when they landed the next day. A couple of days later they were ready to fly, and I gave them a run-down on British weather patterns and air traffic control procedures. I suggested to the squadron commander, Joe, that he spent a full week practising instrument flying. When I showed him some typical synoptic met charts, he took the point avidly. In due course I told Joe that, if I was to be any good, he had better let me evaluate the P-47, to which he agreed.

I climbed aboard and found an armchair and a hundred instruments and warning lights, which meant nothing to me. There was also a urinating tube, as in all US aircraft; perhaps the prostates of their airmen go for a burton at an early age. (I piloted Canberras on many occasions for over eight hours, but I never needed a piddle.) I sorted out the essential instruments, such as the fuel gauges, the boost gauge, the coolant and engine temperature, taxied out and took off. She was as lethargic as a sleepy lion as the engine struggled to get this barrel up to flying speed. As I was about to run out of runway I hauled back on the stick in desperation, and she reluctantly lifted into the air. I retracted the undercart and kept low to gain flying speed ahead of the climb, nearly removing some of Chichester cathedral in the process. At about 300 mph I put her into a battle climb and she grumbled her way up to 30,000 feet. Then I aerobated her, using every manoeuvre in the book and some which I had learned on my own. She was swift as a striking cobra with the ailerons, but even by pulling full gee not tight enough for my liking. I turned her on her back, went into a vertical dive, and almost immediately attempted to get out of it. I throttled right back, but she stuck in the dive. I had to use both hands to haul her out with all my strength, even so I lost 15,000 feet in the process. As I came out of the dive I used my zoom speed to do some vertical rolls; and she rolled quick as a Catherine wheel eight times before she began to run out of flying speed.

I lost height and joined the airfield circuit, only to realize that I didn't know her stalling speed at ground level. I had made stalling tests at height, but an aircraft stalls more quickly in rarified air. But no matter, she was heavy, fat, and her acceleration was poor, so I made some calculations, selected undercart down, gave her fifteen degrees of flap on the final turn, and drove her in at 135 mph. Then I put down full flaps, left the throttle where it was allowing the extra drag to reduce the air speed. I throttled right back a hundred yards from the runway threshold and she touched down on three points neat as a virgin. She didn't need much brakes because the flap area created a great deal of drag, and I steered her to her parking lot where a NCO helped me to get unstrapped.

'Say, Sir, that was a might fine landing,' he said.

'Not bad, Chief, for my first time up in one of these birds,' I replied.

'You foist time up! Whadyamean? Ain't you flown a P-47 before?'

'No, Chief. One bird's very much like another.'

News travels fast, and when I went to see Joe he was chainsmoking cigars and talking to himself.

'You ain't never flown a P-47 before?' he muttered.

'Never, Joe,' I assured him.

'Jesus Christ! This could get me put in the cooler. All pilots in the USAAF have to attend a month's course on the engine, instruments and all that crap. Then another month being taught the effects of the controls etcetera in flight simulators. Before they make their first solo they have to have a chat with the padre after they've written out their Wills. There's a special technique needed to get the bird unstuck from the ground, for example.'

'I got it unstuck OK,' I said, 'but it was a bit tough.'

'Then you've got to be spot on for the landing,' he drooled on. 'If not you finish up in a furnace. Goddam it!

47

I'd better check that.' And he yelled for help. 'Chief,' he said, 'get that bird flown by this officer checked for a heavy landing.'

'No need, Sir,' he replied. 'I saw the landing and it was perfect in all respects.'

Joe gazed at me. 'Say what are you, a bloody conjurer?'

'No, I just fly by the seat of my pants. Now have you got an hour to spare?'

I then explained that the Thunderbolt would be useless in an interceptor role. Its rate of climb was much too low, it lacked the necessary acceleration, and its expansive turning circle made it vulnerable. Some of these faults could be eradicated if the petrol tanks were only half filled ahead of the scramble, but that seemed to be a negative approach. The heavy bombers of the US Eighth Army Air Force were beginning probing attacks into German air space, but they were relying on their massive internal armament and it wouldn't work. When the Luftwaffe worked out new tactics, these heavy, unescorted bombers would be massacred. The bomber commanders would scream for long range fighter escorts, and the P-47 would do that very well. However, it should not be flown alongside the bombers, but at combat cruising speed. This would mean that wing after wing of escorts would take off at synchronized times on the same course as the bombers, fly above them and turn for base when fuel availability made it necessary, all the time sweeping the skies for German fighters. Other wings would do likewise until the bombers arrived within escort range of Fighter Command. I said that in my view the demand would be for the P-47s to carry even more fuel as the ambitions of bombers grew, when they would attempt to select targets deeper and deeper inside Germany.

When I had finished my monologue, Joe shook his head.

'How the hell am I going to put that to the top brass?' he enquired. 'They dictate policy not bloody squadron commanders.'

'They think they dictate policy,' I said, 'but they've got their heads so far stuffed up their arses they can't think of anything. Here, give me some paper and I'll draft a signal for your Commanding General with a copy to the Pentagon.'

'Jeezuz! A copy to the Pentagon! I'd get red-hot buckshot up my ass!'

'Get off it, Joe. I've done it hundreds of times. Mark it Most Immediate and give it a Top Secret classification. They always sit up and take notice when they get one of those.'

I don't know what the effect of Joe's signal was, but within a couple of weeks Joe got his marching orders. He was to redeploy his squadron to the East Anglian area, where the force of heavy bombers was being increased in size daily, to train in bomber escort tactics. In which context it is important to keep in mind the part played by the US P-51, the Mustang.

The Americans designed the P-51 as a single-seater fighter, evaluated it and found it to be useless. They accordingly sold some to the RAF in order to make room in their maintenance hangars for other types. I took every opportunity of test-flying new types, and at one of the stations where I was based there was a maintenance unit which, I discovered, possessed a number of P-51s. The Boss of the MU wanted some P-51s test flown, but none of the pilots on the station had flown the marque, so I suggested I would test-fly a few. The aircraft was powered by the American Allison engine, not that that meant anything to me at the time. I took off and reached 2,000 feet, whereupon the engine stopped dead. I cursed, turned off the fuel supply and glided back to the runway, leaving it to the last moment before selecting flaps and undercarriage down. We called this a 'dead stick' landing. They towed me back to the hangar and I told the MU people to make a strip inspection of the engine. Then I took off in another and made 5,000 feet before the engine cut out, which gave me room to make a tidier dead sticker. They brought out the tractor and towed me to the hangar, where I climbed aboard a third P-51. This one took me to 10,000 feet, but I stayed above the airfield while I practised aerobatics before the engine cut out.

Again I made a dead stick landing, and I told the Boss of the MU to ground all P-51s until the manufacturers of the engine had made strip inspections and reported on what modifications were required. I thought very deeply about the Mustang which was a larger fighter than the Spitfire and it had clean business-like lines. In the short time I had to aerobat it I thought it handled very well, but leaving aside the unreliability of the engine, it was grossly underpowered. I sent a note to higher authority suggesting that experiments should be made in fitting it with a Rolls-Royce Merlin engine. Whether my appeal influenced any decision or not I don't know, but the Mustang Mk 1V was fitted with a Merlin and it transformed the aircraft. The USAAF were given licences to construct the Packard Merlin in the USA, and thousands were soon coming off the production lines. As I had prognosticated, in 1944 the USAAF were demanding more and more long range escorts; they even demanded that the Spitfire should be given that role, which was impossible – it would have taken two years to remodel the Spitfire. Then the Yanks fitted their Mustangs and Thunderbolts with extra long range tanks, which gave the Mustang in particular the radius of action to fly to Berlin and back. Joe's Thunderbolts were good old war horses, but the Mustang reigned supreme.

CHAPTER 9

RAF stations are normally sited in rural areas and are considered a darned nuisance by the people living locally. Over the take off and landing zones aircraft are noisy at low level, and farmers' cattle tend to scatter, shooting parties are disturbed, and so on. This did not apply so much in war, but I always tried to keep the neighbours sweet when I received complaints. On the other hand, in a surprising number of respects the RAF can help the neighbours. One day I received an interesting invitation. The owner of a large estate to the north of Tangmere explained that he had inherited his land on condition that he maintained the herd of deer that went with it. The trouble was that the deer were breaking through the fences and giving trouble to the neighbouring farmers. I went to see him and explore the lie of the land, and he suggested a weekly cull of three deer, one of which he would give to the farmers, I could keep one, and he would share the third with friends. We walked over the affected area, and it was clear that rifles were out of the question, for the bullets would carry much too far. I said I would sort out the armament and the tactics and he, in turn, was to put up red flags between the hours of ten and twelve every Saturday morning.

The squadrons worked seven days a week, of course, but Saturday was as good a day as any.

By this time I had established clay pigeon ranges at all the airfields, after careful tuition in safety precautions, and shotguns and cartridges were issued from the station armouries when properly authorized. I invited the two New Zealand squadrons to let me have half a dozen pilots every Saturday morning for 'extra gunnery training purposes'. Almost to a man they had shot deer in their native country, and we worked out our *modus operandi*. Together with gangs of airmen, we would collect together on the farmers' land and drive stray animals towards the fences which enclosed the main herd. The guns would walk with the drivers, and it was important to keep the line straight. The guns were given only a limited arc of fire ahead. We had no buckshot, but the Kiwis had the answer. The caps of the skeet shooting cartridges were removed and candle grease was poured in, which more or less solidified the pellets. Firing out of range would not be tolerated, and the point of aim was to be the neck behind the head.

We killed three deer in no time on our first sortie, and our chaps dragged one off to our lorries while I was talking to the land-owner whose men were dealing with his. He was delighted and hoped we could make it a weekly event, and I said we would try because it was a pleasant change of routine for my chaps – nor would the venison be anything but acceptable.

When I arrived at our parking area, I found that the Kiwis had already skinned our deer, and were busy doing a professional job butchering it. I gave them a ticking off, and they replied that this was the way they did it in New Zealand. I told them they weren't in bloody New Zealand now, so next time they would leave the beast intact. Every week I sold the Officers Mess a carcass for the price of a pint of beer to all the airmen involved. And I reserved the right to be given a slice of venison for my own home consumption. I bet there weren't many RAF stations other than Tangmere which contained haunch of venison on the menu!

I rented a cottage in the middle of Tangmere itself, and my wife joined me. It was a typical West Sussex flint cottage up a quiet lane which led onto agricultural land where we could exercise our dogs. Incongruously, my wife had a bad-tempered old Pekinese and I had an enormous white bull-terrier by name Crippen. They got on very well after an initial encounter when the Peke attempted to hypnotize Crippen by glaring at him unblinkingly with its luminous eyes. The bull-terrier stood it for a few minutes, and then leapt at the Peke, but I grabbed him by the collar before he could enclose the little brute's neck with his jaws and toss the carcass over his head. My wife had hysterics, so I gave Crippen a severe ticking-off. The Peke saw reason and never attempted to play silly buggers again. Indeed, if another dog tried anything on the Peke, I well know that Crippen would have murdered it.

Tangmere itself contained a medieval church, and in the graveyard a number of British and German pilots and aircrew lay buried. There was one general purpose store and about fifty cottages. Chichester was three miles away, and my wife bicycled there periodically for the shopping. On one occasion, as she was returning, a couple of fighter/bomber Messerschmitts attempted a rhubarb attack on the airfield. A man walking by the main road saw them as my wife was passing, pushed her into a ditch and jumped in after her. The bombs exploded hundreds of yards away, but he showed quick reactions. Tangmere was handmade for rhubarb operations, and our ground defences were on nothing like the scale of the Germans. I am surprised that so few attacks were made for the airfield was only a couple of miles from the sea.

The parish priest had been honorary chaplain to the station since it became operational in 1926. Padre Hurn was a splendid man. There were no formal Church parades in the war, but Padre Hurn's beautiful little church was open day and night, and a full range of services was held every Sunday. He was always available for advice, but he did most of his work visiting his parishoners, the squadron dispersals and technical hangars. He had a little black Austin 7 which was constantly seen bouncing round the perimeter tracks, regular as the NAAFI van. Civilians were not authorized to drive on the airfield without special authority, which was freely given to the padre who knew how to keep out of the way of taxiing aircraft better than most. There were no Mess ceremonies in the war, but after the war Padre Hurn always attended formal dinners in the Officers Mess, opening proceedings by saying grace. Nor was he averse to a tipple of sherry and wine, but considering the number of drinks wished on him he drank modestly. No one told me when he died, but my guess is that he served Tangmere for forty years.

The Mess Secretary was another old hand, a retired Squadron Leader by name Bill Barrell. His job was to allocate rooms to incoming officers, supervise the batmen who were under the aegis of the Head Batman, Tom Griffiths. Tom was a civilian who had been serving at Tangmere in the more spacious pre-war days, and there were a few other regular civilians. RAF batmen were in the majority because of the vastly increased demands for rooms as the officer strength increased. All save senior officers lived two to a room, something unheard of before the war. And consider that each of the three satellite stations had its own Mess. Bill would also keep an eye on the Mess Steward, Paddy O'Brien, another pre-war civilian. Paddy could be best described as the *maître d'hôtel*, acting as Mess butler, ensuring that the dining tables were properly laid and the waiters got a move on, maintaining a smooth liaison between the kitchens and the serving area. Outside, Job Wilkins, the Head Gardener, tended the Mess gardens, the grass and flower beds single-handed, cursing because his gardeners had been called up, and his beloved playing fields had been converted into farm land.

Things were made no easier because of the loss of one wing of the building during the Luftwaffe raid early in the war, but standards were high. In theory, the Mess Committee represented the higher management of this sizeable hotel, with the President of the Mess Committee (PMC) in overall charge, but in war these duties were carried out by the permanent staff. Little did I know that I would be made the PMC in a few years.

I normally had lunch at whatever airfield I was working at, but I did not forget our domestic diet. I always took with me in my RAF car a twelve-bore shotgun and a .22 rifle with a telescopic sight. Returning from places like Ford, I would drive through the lanes keeping a careful eye open. A covey of patridge was easy enough to pick out in season, which was a task for the rifle. I would aim at the one in the middle, and when he suddenly keeled over, the others would gang around to take a look. This gave me time to bag another, sometimes three before the remainder decided to push off. Nor was I averse to collecting a brace of pheasants when the larder demanded. The occasional hare came in handy, and rabbits also helped to feed the dogs. Roosting pigeons in trees were easy meat; I would merely stop under the tree, aim vertically out of the window and they would drop on the car. If times were hard, I would shoot green plover from the flocks that inhabited the airfield and were a minor danger to aircraft. As dusk fell, the squadrons would be released for the night, and I would drive over Tangmere airfield on the *qui vive*. The plover would take off as my car approached, but not soon enough to stop me collecting a couple of brace with a right and left. Golden plover were, of course, protected, but the green bedded down on the airfield in their thousands. They were too small for me to be bothered to pluck them, so I skinned them which automatically removed the feathers. A couple of plover per person made for a decent meal.

We scarcely suffered from wartime food rationing; indeed, we had enough to entertain selected guests.

CHAPTER 10

A flight of Lysanders was based on a discreet part of the airfield, and no one was supposed to know what they were there for. When I commanded a Special Duty squadron, it was equipped with Lysanders among other marques and I frequently flew the type. It was a high wing monoplane with a radial Bristol engine, originally intended for Army courier duties. It was, however, hopelessly vulnerable in battlefield conditions. By modifying the cockpit it could carry a pilot and two or three passengers and baggage, and it had a short take off and landing capability on rough fields. In flight it made very little noise, and was termed the 'whispering bat'.

At first I wondered what a flight of Lysanders was doing at Tangmere, especially as the pilots did not use the Officers Mess. They messed in a large cottage directly opposite the main gates of the station, and were shadowy figures. Camouflage netting covered the aircraft by day, and save for the occasional flight test they flew only by night. I happened to bump into an officer I had known before the war and asked him what he was doing at Tangmere. He waved his hand vaguely and said he was attached to the Lysander flight. I then remembered that he had been up at Oxford before the war studying modern languages, with the intention of joining the Diplomatic Corps. This completed the jigsaw.

I was aware that British and French agents were being dropped in France to assist in forming the various resistance groups, popularly known as the Maquis, under the aegis of the Special Operations Executive (SOE), and it became clear that the Lysanders were involved in this. It was very much a cloak and dagger operation and the pilots had to be most discreet. I didn't know how to contact my friend, so I slipped a note through the letter-box of their Mess inviting him to come to supper and to bring a friend along. They did and were given a distinctly gamey meal, much to their satisfaction. Obviously, they didn't talk shop, nor did my wife and I ask any probing questions, and the atmosphere became more and more relaxed. They enjoyed a change of scene outside the confines of their Mess, where they could lower their guard.

In short time it became a regular event for different members of the flight to come in and help dispose of the game which was so easily available to me, and they provided highly entertaining company, quite different from the ordinary run of the mill on the station. Better not to mention names, but Hugh Verity wrote a book about his experiences, *We Flew by Moonlight,* and he was a regular visitor. So was John Hunt, a leading concert pianist, who died in harness in Toyko some years ago. In my cottage was a battered old piano, and half the keys didn't work. Nothing dismayed, John would put on a brilliant performance pushing out Chopin's Nocturnes with the utmost delicacy and apparently no effort, although some of the piano keys only worked when I hit them with a hammer. Years after the war I played around in the Foreign Office and visited every British embassy in the world. One of my cloak and dagger friends was an ambassador in a faraway place, and he gave me a decent dinner in return for the stuff I had handed out to him.

The SOE pilots were strictly hand-picked in all senses of the expression – certainly those based on Tangmere were. They were Oxbridge graduates, fluent in French and possibly other languages. Surprisingly enough, RAF pilots were not tested or categorized as to the quality of their night vision which can differ widely even though daylight vision is first class, but I feel sure that such tests must have been applied before selection for SOE duties. There was no need for them to be rated exceptional pilots on selection since there is nothing difficult in flying a Lysander. But after passing the *ab initio* stage they were given rigorous training in specialized flying techniques, and their resourcefulness was tested to the full.

When not in the field, secret agents were housed elsewhere, but when their turn to be landed in occupied territory came, they would be given their final briefing. They might have to remain in occupied Europe for months or years, but they had the facility to ask for an early recall if, for example, the Gestapo was getting wind of them. Airfields other than Tangmere were used where Lockheed Hudsons were based, which had a much longer range and could carry a much greater payload in which armaments and general military hardware were included. Concentrating on the Tangmere operations, the agent and his or her wireless operator would be driven to the Mess after dusk when good enough weather conditions were forecast. The moon should not be totally obscured by cloud and good visibility was at a premium.

BBC overseas broadcasts were one of the main sources to confirm that the drop would continue as planned. A simple message at the prearranged time such as: 'Your Aunt Anna's cat is dead' would suffice, spoken in French of course. Plans would have been already put in train for the drop. The Maquis selected a suitable field in a safe area and transmitted its whereabouts by devious means to SOE. Often, agents due to return would be kept in hiding nearby, moving from one 'safe' house to another. French VIPs wishing to defect to the Free French HQ in the UK might be among them. When the decision to go was taken, the agent and his wireless operator were driven from the SOE cottage to the waiting Lysander at night to embark. The W/T set was contained in a heavy suitcase.

The pilot took off in the dark on the grass – no runway lights thank-you! – and would proceed on course at sea-level. No R/T transmissions by the pilot were permitted. On making landfall he flew on a dead reckoning course together with map reading to his target. Map reading by day is none too easy, even if obvious landmarks every five minutes on the route are circled, and by night I would find it impossible. The pilot would continue at low level overland, and when the Maquis heard the noise of the engine they would shine torches upwards to indicate a flare path, also an arrow to help the pilot land upwind. The incoming agent and his WOP would be rushed away to a safe house, and the returning team would embark. After a hurried briefing by the leader of this element of the Maquis, coupled with any verbal messages the pilot had to give him, the Lysander would take off and vanish into the night en route for Tangmere. On arrival, the returning agents were whisked away by car for debriefing.

This was positively hair-raising stuff, with the ever present possibilities of being shot down by light flak, or of landing at decoy fields held by the German Secret Services who had tortured the Maquis into disclosing the plan. Accidents could happen – all single engine aircraft can only force land if the engine fails. Sometimes the fields selected were inadequate. Trees might obscure the landing area, for example. On one occasion a Lysander's oleo leg stuck into mud to such an extent that the propeller almost hit the ground. It could not be manhandled from the rut, and after an all too lengthy wait a tractor was eventually brought along to haul it out. I remember being scrambled on an interception course towards France at first light. The only instruction I was given was not to open fire indiscriminately. I found a Lysander scurrying for home, over the Channel, having crossed the French coast just before dawn broke. Perhaps this was the one which got stuck in the mud, but whatever the reason it was clear the pilot had been delayed at his dropping field. I escorted it back to Tangmere, much to the relief of the pilot, no doubt.

I was aware that a friend of mine had been involved in such activities and suggested that she wrote a book about it. She had been educated in France and was not yet twenty when taken on by the SOE. On one drop she discovered to her horror that her American wireless operator had not a word of French! She refused point-blank to write about her experiences. 'Every time I think about it,' she said, 'I get nightmares.' On the face of it anyway, my SOE pilot friends kept their cool – they most certainly seemed to think it a bit of a lark!

CHAPTER 11

In Chichester there was a pub called the Unicorn, and it looked more like a shoddy mausoleum. Stark as the interior was, the atmosphere was enlivened by mine host, Arthur King. He was of medium height, portly, balding, rotund of face with sparkling eyes, and wore a constant grin. My guess is that he began working as a barrow-boy in the East End and later learned his trade as a bartender. Having become a publican proper, he then found out about catering. He was an astute business man and the Unicorn, large as it was, was managed like clockwork. His banqueting hall was in constant demand by the Free-masons, Rotarians and for civic functions. On these occasions Arthur had no problems about food-rationing. I have little doubt that he made private arrangements with cattle and sheep farmers and with local fishermen. The Unicorn drew the pilots based at Tangmere, Merston and Westhampnett to it like a magnet, and they would swarm in like a horde of locusts after being released from operations. Arthur welcomed them with open arms, not for financial gain for he sold them beer at much reduced prices, but because he genuinely felt a paternal pride in them.

When he called time, the more senior officers, the mafia, would dutifully disappear from the main bar to set an example to their juniors, only to climb the stairs and enter a more secret bar. One merit of drinking in pubs was that it allowed Sergeant Pilots to socialize with officers, whereas otherwise they would have been confined to their separate messes. More often than not, in the secret bar after hours, one would find a sprinkling of police officers knocking back the beer. An hour after legal drinking should have ended, Arthur would call time and escort all and sundry to the main door, lock it and hurry along to open a back door. The mafia would then troop to the Top Secret bar, the sanctum sanctorum, where drinks were on the house. There traditional rites were enacted as, for example, foot-marks on the ceiling. When an officer was decorated for gallantry, provided he was a member of the mafia, his shoes and socks would be torn off, his feet immersed in a bowl of soot mixed with water, and he would be manhandled vertically in an upside-down posture until his feet were near enough to the ceiling for him to stamp on it. When he had recovered he was hoisted up again to sign the ceiling with his footprints. There were some well-known names on that ceiling.

At one time rumour spread that Arthur was a German spy. I knew him very well and this was bloody nonsense. Since I joined the RAF I have had an acute awareness, an extra-sensory perception, of matters involving national security, which I have proved on many occasions, not least when I was with the Foreign Office. In any case the flying leaders had hardly any secrets in their heads worthy of consideration. The simple fact is that Arthur adored his pilots, and had a Walter Mitty image that he was one of them. After D Day when airstrips in Northern France were operational, Tangmere and its satellites were kept busy accepting squadrons returning from France to reorganize, and flying out new units to take their place. Once or twice a week, Arthur would climb aboard a clapped-out Anson and would be flown to airstrips occupied by Tangmere Sector's squadrons. He would bring with him great hampers of delicacies, such as legs of lamb, to add lustre to the pilots' food rations. He made no charge, but they insisted on giving him French wine and cheeses in return, most of which he would hand over to the Officers Mess. He was a great guy, and no account of Tangmere in wartime would be complete without a mention of him.

Drinking in pubs is not my métier, but one had to indulge with officers and other ranks to socialize outside the formal confines of the messes. Tongues wag when lubricated with beer, and any slight grievances mentioned by NCOs and airmen could be rectified the quicker when one was aware of them. But these were stag occasions, and I had a conscience as to my wife's social welfare. It was a stroke of luck, therefore, when I met Mrs Pike, who retained her maiden name, Olive Snell, for professional purposes. She was a portrait painter, and together with other artists a number of her portraits of military men appeared in such glossies as *The Tatler*. NAAFI wagons used to trundle tea and buns around the airfields, and at Tangmere a women's voluntary organization was allowed to drive their vans onto the airfields for the same purpose. I bought a mug of tea one day from a lady and we passed the time of day having a chat. I noted that she was examining my face somewhat critically, then she suddenly said she wanted to paint my portrait. I was somewhat taken aback. She introduced herself and explained that she was not an authorized war artist, but she did hold exhibitions of her work.

My memory clicked, and I recalled a coloured pencil sketch of my mother-in-law in her early teens, dressed in hunting kit, which was drawn before World War I. Even a generation and more later, it bore an incredible likeness to her, and was signed Olive Snell followed by a little squiggle. I told her about it, which excited her since she well remembered the occasion. She had been spending a weekend at my wife's family's ancestral home and had asked particularly if she could sketch my mother-in-law, thus ignoring her four sisters. She wanted to catch up on the news of the family, so she invited my wife and myself to tea. When we got there she decided to do a portrait of my wife as well. Her husband, Ebenezer Pike was there, a marvellous old war-horse, too old to rejoin the colours, after a long career in the Grenadier Guards. As he escorted us to the gate, his sharp eye lighted on my car.

'Y'r bloody car is dirty,' he snorted. 'Officers and gentlemen must keep up the standard. Get y'r soldier servant to wash it.'

Their magnificent mansion above Arundel had been requisitioned by the Army, and they had rented a charming cottage in a village at the foot of the Goodwood Downs. The Duke of Richmond had let Olive have the Shell House as her studio, which is unique to my knowledge. It is the size of a large room, overlooking Goodwood House, ideal for her purpose. As I remember, the exterior was of West Sussex flint, but inside the walls were covered with sea shells and small colourful stones picked up from over the world which glittered like diamonds.

Heaven knows how many generations of young Richmond daughters laboured on this project, but the end result is quite fascinating.

Olive decided to paint me in heavy oils, head and shoulders, and she insisted that I wore flying overalls and my pink flying scarf. The scarf would add colour, she explained, little realizing that it had once been the seventh veil of a seven veil dancer performing at the Chatham Empire. My portrait was not enitrely successful, even though she liked it. Her romantic style ran away with her and the mouth was too effeminate. She painted my wife in profile and that was certainly a success. She hung them both in her exhibitions, and gave them to us when I met her a couple of years later. Mine was photographed and appeared in *The Tatler*, much to my embarrassment.

After a year at Tangmere, it was decided that I should spout the gospel to a wider audience. I was sent to the Staff of HQ No 12 Group, based near Nottingham, in the post as Gunnery/Tactics Officer. Our stations were sited as far north as Newcastle, and to Chester to the nor'west, a large parish indeed. The squadrons were seeing little action, apart from fighter sweeps to Holland and Belgium. Those in the north and the west were virtually training units, taking in newly trained pilots and bringing them up to combat efficiency. This wasn't being done with too much success, and it was my job to improve matters – but fast. This aim was achieved, though it sometimes meant sacking flying leaders who were not up to the mark, and replacing them with officers in need of a rest from operations.

CHAPTER 12

I spent a year at 12 Group HQ, and when it was obvious that Germany was beginning to collapse, my boss, the Air Officer Commanding, called me in. He told me I had done a good job, but he didn't see the point of retaining me on his Staff any longer, with which I wholeheartedly agreed. He pointed out that after Germany was finished with, there would come a demand to start reducing the strength of Fighter Command; pilots who joined for the duration would be given their bowler hats, apart from those selected for extended or regular commissions. How would I like to take command of a squadron?

'I'd like nothing better, Sir,' I replied. 'Which one?'

'No 1 Squadron,' he said.

'Cor blimey!' I spouted involuntarily with glee.

'I thought you'd be pleased,' he smiled. 'Not many are given the honour to command the senior squadron in the RAF. As a matter of fact I've selected you because I see from your reports that you have a considerable ability to evaluate the worth of a squadron. I take it, therefore, that you know how to put one back on the rails again. 1 squadron is badly run down and needs a kick in the arse. Sack anyone you like.'

'I don't like sacking them, Sir,' I said. 'I prefer to drag them up by their hair.'

'Do it your way, then. But do it fast.'

Small wonder the squadron was in a mess! It was based on a primitive airfield with a single runway on top of a Yorkshire moor, named Hutton Cranswick; Beverley was our nearest town, about fifteen miles south. The accommodation for officers and men consisted of wooden shacks and Nissen huts with rusting corrugated iron roofs. There was no hangar, and squadron stores were kept in Nissen huts. When it snows in Yorkshire it is no laughing matter. We had our own snow ploughs and graders to attempt to keep the runway clear, but we had little capacity to spare to tackle the lanes leading down the wolds. Fixing snow blades to our four-wheel drive petrol bowsers was a good idea for the runway, but I was disinclined to see these heavy vehicles toppling down the lanes and vanishing into snow-drifts.

Again, the squadron was equipped with Spitfires Mk XXI, the very latest marque in Fighter Command and far superior in performance to any other fighter in the world, save for the jet-propelled Me 262; but despite its speed advantage, we could have out-manoeuvred it. The Mk XXI was powered by the Rolls-Royce Griffin engine which developed over 2,000 hp, but it required highly sophisticated maintenance. Indeed, merely to remove and replace the engine cowlings, which was necessary on every weekly inspection, at the least took one and a half hours. I know because I checked this with a stop-watch. And this was the only squadron in the Command to have the Mk XXI, so further production of the model would probably come to a halt when the war ended, therefore essential spare parts were difficult to come by. There were two different sorts of Mk XXI on the squadron, one had a five bladed propeller, and the other a pair of three propellers rotating in a contra-propulsion. Before I did much else I decided to fly them to evaluate their respective performances.

The torque on take off in the four bladed Spitfire Mk XIV had been bad enough, and I knew that the five blader would be even more preposterous, especially as it had a much more powerful engine. The cockpit lay-out was slightly more sophisticated than other marques, but not particularly so. I taxied to the runway, swerving from one side to the other to see directly ahead as the nose cowlings obscured forward vision, turned into wind and inched the throttle open. As she gathered speed with more and more throttle, I felt the torque begin to bite. I began to counter the torque with opposite aileron and full rudder, and when she was ready to fly I was using a lot of strength to maintain control. No doubt the tyre accepting the weight of torque was flat as a pancake. In no time at all I had enough speed to start a steep climb and she soared up to 35,000 feet in record time. I played with her and she was the same as the old Mk I in handling characteristics, if rather more agile. She easily exceeded 400 mph on the descent with a lot of power to spare, and her approach and touch down speed was about 10 mph higher than other models because of her extra weight.

I then climbed into the contra-prop which had exactly the same cockpit lay-out. There was no torque whatsoever on take off because three propellers countered the other three. She was faster on the climb than the five blader because of the extra thrust granted by the sixth blade. She soared up to 45,000 feet with more in her than that, but she was slower on the dive than the five blader because the sixth blade created a certain amount of drag at near terminal velocity. On my way back to the dispersal I pondered over the two aircraft. If they took off in formation, one pilot would be fighting the torque, but the other would have no such problem. Furthermore, some dummkopf might forget which of them he was flying and not take corrective action against the torque of the five blader in the belief that he was in a contraprop, in which case he'd finish up in a ball of fire when the aircraft flicked onto its back after getting airborne. I gave orders that red sticky labels be stuck on the windshield, reminding pilots which type they were flying.

I took time to get to know the Senior NCOs and discuss their problems, talking to them about their troubles whether professional or domestic. I am a skilled marriage counsellor and long after I left whatever unit it was, I used to receive letters from NCOs and airmen I barely remembered. Their morale was low mainly because of lack of concern by the officers, and they freely admitted that this had spread down to the airmen. Very little flying was being achieved mainly because it didn't seem to have been called for by the squadron commander and his flight commanders. Several aircraft were permanently unserviceable on minor inspections for want of spares; although new parts had been indented for, little seemed to happen.

A minor inspection is a misnomer. It was necessary for an aircraft to be given such an inspection after it had flown a hundred hours. The upper and lower engine cowlings were removed, the engine was gone over with a fine toothcomb; all pipes were examined for wear as were electric cables; the magnetoes were retuned and so on. As to the fuselage, all inspection hatches were removed and the cable controls were examined for chafing; the rivets holding the fuselage to the members were counted; the main spars were carefully examined for signs of cracking; the ailerons were checked to ensure the droop did not exceed the limits, and the rest. The aircraft was jacked up and the under-carriage was retracted and lowered time and time again while the system was examined. The radio fitters would replace the R/T set for inspection. The cannon and machine-guns were cleaned, greased and harmonized with the gun-sight, the instrument fitters went to work and the tyres were changed. Even the pilot's seat was removed and the cockpit cleaned with vacuum hoses.

This was called a minor inspection to differentiate from a major inspection, which took place after 250 hours flight. The only real difference between the two was that it was mandatory to replace certain components with new ones at this stage – the magnetoes, for example. These aside, there were daily inspections, before and after flight, weekly and monthly inspections. As to minor and major inspections it is plain to see that, if every aircraft flew the same number of hours as the rest, then after a hundred flying hours all the Spitfires would be unserviceable at the same time waiting minor inspections. The way to avoid this was to stagger the flying hours per aircraft so that ideally only one aircraft would be due for a minor or major inspection at any one time, thereby allowing the whole maintenance force to deal with it; when the job was finished another Spitfire would be ready to be taken off the line. But to achieve this, under the squadron comman-der's overall supervision, the flight commanders should co-ordinate the flying hours per aircraft in co-operation with their Senior Technical NCOs.

I nearly burst a blood vessel when I learned that no such practice was being implemented. It was so obvious!

CHAPTER 13

I next passed the time of day with the airmen, who were a disgruntled lot. There was little social life for them; the food was bloody awful; the hint was dropped that the officers didn't bother much with them; they were under-employed because there was not enough flying going on; and those on the maintenance side were held up for lack of spares. It was a dismal catalogue. Most of them were anxious to be demobbed, but a few showed interest in staying on in the RAF, improving their skills and making a career of it.

'Well, you won't get demobbed until Japan gives in,' I

told them. 'But that may happen sooner than you think. The Yanks have sunk their fleet and are setting light to all their cities with bloody gréat oil incendiaries. Meantime I'll get you some work to do and try to improve your lot. Incidentally, how would you like to go to sunny Sussex by the sea?'

There was a murmur of interest, broken by a broad Yorkshire voice. 'Ah've never 'eard of bloody Sussex,' it announced. 'If I want to see the sea, ah go to bloody Scarborough.'

'You might be surprised.' I said. 'Sussex girls are very willing. Meanwhile, the Corporals are to get their hair cut and then detail men to do likewise. Warn the camp barber to sharpen his scissors. You're going on parade.'

I walked out of the hut and shut the door to hear a swell of discontent arise. 'Fooking parades', 'I haven't been on parade since after I joined up', 'Sodding tin soldiers', and so forth. As a matter of fact I disliked parades and ceremonial intensely, and after first recruitment into the RAF, officers and men did not parade during the war. However, at the heart of it, parades and ceremonial are essential to a disciplined military service. They make men smarten themselves up, straighten their backs, and ensure that their uniforms are pressed and their buttons clean. Above all, the chain of command is displayed for all to see; the senior officer is obviously the boss, his senior subordinates do what they are told on the dot, and junior officers are cut down to size. SNCOs show their authority over Corporals, who in turn indicate to the men that they wield power. The rank of Corporal is important and difficult to hold down; an exceptional Corporal could rise to the highest rank in the RAF. On the other hand they eat and drink with the airmen where it is all too easy to allow undue familiarity to denigrate the rank. On the other, the men sleep in dormitories, whereas a Corporal has a private room in that dormitory and is in charge of the cleanliness and tidiness of it. Airmen are mechanics, but Corporals can become fitters provided they pass the exams.

I had already seen enough of the officers in the Mess to have a good enough appreciation of their worth. A few had a high potential, some were average, the rest had no potential to speak of. I was puzzled by my senior flight commander, who was, after all, my second in command. He had been awarded the DFC in action, and had been shot down and interned in a POW camp, where he became a leading member of the Escape Committee. Such bodies co-ordinated the attempts of would-be escapees to ensure that the plans made by one officer would not compromise those of another. And when prisoners did escape, security at the camp would be tightened to the extent that other attempts would be more hazardous until the hue and cry cooled. This officer, Bert, had eventually made his own escape, and for his overall efforts had been awarded the MBE.

However, there was something obviously wrong with him, so I called him into my office and sat him down.

'How do you like the Spitfire Mk XXI?' I enquired.

He remained silent, and then blurted it out. 'I've never flown one, Sir,' he said.

I raised my eyebrows. 'How come? How long have you been on the squadron?'

'Three months. I was shot down on my last flight, and I feel sick at the idea of taking off again.'

'Perfectly understandable. I've been shot down on more occasions than you, and it was always a bit of a sweat to get airborne next time. But we can easily resolve this problem. I'll put you in a contraprop this afternoon, sit in the caravan and give you a bit of dual over the R/T.'

He blanched. 'Hadn't I better go to a conversion unit

and get in some dual with an instructor before I fly a Spitfire?'

'No,' I replied. 'You'll take off this afternoon, like it or lump it. That's an order. If you disobey, I'll mark you down as LMF (lacking in moral fibre) and have you remustered to ground duties. How would you like to be an Equipment Officer?'

He didn't like, and that afternoon I strapped him into a contraprop, reminded him of the instrument panel, told him the approach and landing speed, informed him that there would be no torque on take off, so the rudder bias should be set to neutral, and instructed him to stay aloft for an hour on a cross-country flight, return over base and perform medium level aerobatics which I would observe, approach to land, overshoot from the landing and touch down next time.

I followed him in my car as he taxied out, watched him take off, then climbed into the caravan. It was managed by a Corporal who controlled aircraft moving on the ground, on take off and landing. If he saw two aircraft taxiing in such directions that they might collide with each other, he would order the pilots to halt and sort out the mess. If he saw a pilot approaching with his undercart retracted, he would warn him over the R/T and shoot off a red Very light – all manner of things. I told the Corporal to brew up some tea as I would be taking over from him for an hour. I called up Bert and asked him if he was OK, he said he was but he didn't sound very enthusiastic. He returned to base at about 15,000 feet and performed a few adequate barrel rolls and steep turns, but I noted that he wasn't prepared to loop the loop. Then he began his descent and joined the circuit, selected undercart down on the down wind leg, and made his turn onto the final approach. He was too high and too close to the runway, but I left him alone as he was to overshoot before touching down. As he climbed away, I told him that he had made a balls of it, that he was to turn on finals at 700 feet, a mile from the runway threshold, continue his descent at 130 mph with fifteen degrees of flap, and select full flap 500 yards from the runway threshold. He was 5 mph too fast when he landed on one wheel, and she bounced awkwardly but not dangerously, then she settled down on three points.

I met him as he climbed out of the cockpit, and he was quite composed. He told me that he had been rough with the controls and tended to overcorrect, but he had regained his confidence. I said he was to fly two sorties a day to iron out the creases, and in a couple of week's time I would take him up for a dogfight and some formation aerobatics. He looked as wan as I felt when I mentioned formation aerobatics. I had already been involved in a mid-air collision and didn't much like the prospect of another!

The squadron adjutant was Tom Black, a Flight Lieutenant and an experienced pilot. He was in for the war which had disrupted his apprenticeship intended to make him a master plumber, and he had splayed thumbs presumably from pushing putty. He was a shrewd devil, rough in his mannerisms and with a chip on his shoulder, but he was a first class organizer. He supervised the Orderly Room which contained a Corporal and a couple of clerks, where the squadron files were maintained and the bumf was shuffled, although he kept in flying practice. He was an awkward customer, but before long we were on easy terms.

Then there was the Flight Sergeant i/c Discipline, a stupid title because he was the equivalent of a Regimental Sergeant Major. I called him in and there was a thunderous knock on the door which was quietly opened, quietly closed, followed by a stamping about turn, a march towards my desk, a crash as the figure hit his boots on the floor, a salute which would have done credit to a RSM in the Brigade of Guards, and an announcement;

'Flight Sergeant Miller reporting, SIR!'

'At ease, Flight. I suppose they call you Dusty, having a name like Miller?'

'Aye, they do, Sir, though my real name is Angus.'

'It had occurred to me that you were a bloody Scot,' I said. 'Take a pew, Dusty.'

He sat down, removed his cap and raised his eyebrows.

'Dinna fash,' I said. 'I won't be calling you Dusty outside this office. And for God's sake don't sit at attention, sit at ease. What do you think of the squadron?'

'Hardly for me to say, Sir,' he replied hesitantly.

'Yes it is. I asked the question.'

'Very good, Sir. If you want my opinion, candidly they're a bloody shower. They all want a kick up the backside.'

'There are good and bad 'uns,' I said. 'Living and working conditions don't help. But I'm going to give them the short sharp shock treatment. For the whole of next week the squadron is to parade at 0730 hours in best blue for one hour.'

'Christ!' he muttered. 'Most of the bastards haven't been on parade since their initial acceptance into the RAF.'

'I'm not expecting miracles,' I said. 'I just want a decent turn out. You will give the officers drill practice after work for half an hour, and for the rest of this week. We'll take it easy on uniform inspection for the first three parades, and toughen it up for the next three. Put defaulters on painting everything that doesn't move. I'll brief the officers, and you muster the NCOs and men this evening; the Adjutant will brief them. Any questions?'

'No, Sir!' he exclaimed, rising to his feet, replacing his

cap, and standing to attention. 'If I may say so, I'm behind you and pushing. With your authority we'll soon clean up this shower.'

'That's what I'm here for, Dusty,' I said. 'Now shove off.'

CHAPTER 14

Despite Dusty's bawling and cursing, the first two parades were as bad as I expected them to be. The men were out of line, there were too many bent backs, and half of them were out of step. Before the third parade I warned them that if there wasn't a radical improvement, I would continue the parades for a further week. On the fifth parade they weren't too bad, but I told them it looked as if they were heading for a further week of parades unless they made a supreme effort on the morrow. Then we really went to town on their turn-out. I walked between the files followed by the flight commander concerned, who was followed by Dusty and then the Adjutant. Every man was scrupulously inspected from head to toe, front and back. I would point my finger if I was facing a bad 'un, or tap him on the back if I was looking at him from the rear. Dusty would write my objections in his note-book, and they followed this sort of pattern. Boots, or buttons – meaning not cleaned properly. Scruffy – meaning uniform not pressed sufficiently well. Cap – whereupon Dusty would adjust the forage cap to the correct angle of rake, making menacing noises as he did so. From the rear, it would be hair – meaning it was in need of cutting. Boots – meaning they were down at heel. Uniform not brushed – meaning that it was hairy, or covered with dandruff, or just dusty. The standard punishment for these offences was seven days on fatigue duties, when they would work on peeling potatoes, painting various objects, cleaning out their dormitories and so on.

Curiously enough, much as I disliked them, after parading on consecutive days I felt a sense of camaraderie with those trooping behind or ahead of me. It was a feeling of all being in the same boat so put your heart in it. You could even smell the men around you, and the rhythm of marching with the steady tramping of feet caused a mild sense of hypnosis and elation. I was not altogether surprised, therefore, that the final parade was really very good by the standards of the day. Certainly they did not want another week of it, so they exceeded themselves in order to avoid that. There were a few defaulters – there always are – but in the main their turn-out was first class. After inspecting the ranks I stood them at ease and addressed them, saying that they had rallied very well, but they were to keep up those standards. The main purpose of all of us was to keep the Spitfires flying, and it was up to the pilots to fly them properly. But all in all success depended on team-work, so team-work it would be. On my side I would do all in my power to improve the food and living standards, and take better care of the welfare of other ranks. Finally, when I considered that No 1 squadron was fit enough to claim its place as the senior squadron in the RAF, they might be in for a pleasant surprise.

Meanwhile, things had been happening on the maintenance front. I had seen the Station Equipment Officer together with my Senior Technical NCO and asked him the position regarding the various spare parts we had indented for. He was somewhat lethargic, and muttered that the factory didn't have them, or they were on their way to the nearest Maintenance Unit, or in the pipe-line. Now, demands from units for spares constantly flow through the pipe-line and varying degrees of priority are

76

given to each item. The top priority is marked 'For immediate delivery. Squadron non-operational.' This, of course is rare and normally occurs when a particular part is found faulty on all aircraft through design error or a shorter working life than predicted. I had already gone into a huddle with my engineer over tactics, and I told the Equipment wallah that the squadron would shortly be made unserviceable as a hairline crack had been found on an aileron balancer. I had been in touch with Group HQ, and the AOC had instructed me to make immediate demands for replacements, and for that matter all out-standing spares. I had been told in strict secrecy that the squadron was to be ready for special duties within three weeks. He swallowed the addled egg, but he had to attach special forms to the indents, marked in red 'Squadron non-operational. Immediate' and sign them.

When he had finished I suggested he came with me and I would show him a hair-line crack, and we piled into my car leaving my engineer behind.

'There's one,' I said, placing my finger on the spot.

'I can't see anything,' he announced.

'Give him a magnifying glass,' I said to an NCO.

He peered at the spot.

'My God!' he exclaimed. 'So there is. I don't know how your chaps manage to spot things like that.'

'It's part of the job,' I explained. 'If an aileron balancer broke up through metal fatigue, the aircraft would go into an uncontrollable spin. There'd be small hope for a pilot to bale out with the forces of a spin.'

Someone drove him back to his office.

'Better leave that bit of hair stuck on, Sergeant,' I said. 'The bugger might come back and have another look.'

The senior engineer NCO turned up.

'Got them?' I enquired.

He pulled out of his pocket a sheaf of 'Squadron non-operational. Immediate' forms, which he had pinched from the Equipment Officer's desk.

'Let me remind you of the forms,' I said. 'If the servicing of an aircraft is held up through lack of essential spares, indent for them and I'll forge his signature on the priority label. You and your gang will borrow white coats from the cooks and drive a lorry to the factory warehouse we decided on. You say you are from the Maintenance Unit and want immediate delivery over the counter. OK.'

'Yes, Sir. But what about the accounting? And what will we do with all the bloody aileron balancers we don't want when they arrive?'

'It will take the accounting a couple of years to filter through,' I explained. 'And when we leave this dump, just return the balancers to stores and let them sort it out.'

To be an effective squadron commander, it is essential that one is a better 'scrounger' than one's NCOs. Scrounging is not dissimilar to Chinese stealing. A Chinese servant takes one of his master's valuables and hides it. If, after three months, his master doesn't notice it is missing, then it belongs to the servant. If another squadron with the same type of aircraft is based on the same station, it is fair game to send along a gang of men to the opposition's hangar in the dead of night. There, they find an aircraft stripped for a minor inspection, remove the necessary spare part and put it on my aircraft which is languishing in need of it. On the other hand, I took certain precautions such as bribing the RAF Police with irregular bottles of whisky to make frequent patrols of my hangar during the night. My trick in the case mentioned above rose to the pinnacle of the scrounger's art. It contained elements of conmanship, also gross breaches in the regulations, and of course my gangs went on to use the cooks' white coats technique whenever necessary.

The spares arrived in short time, and I reinforced the maintenance crews with fitters and mechanics from the men working on the front line aircraft to shift the unserviceable Spitfires in a hurry. I also had a meeting with the flight commanders, the Senior Technician and an officer appointed to be general co-ordinator to arrange that flying hours per aircraft should be staggered to suit the maintenance production line. Graphs were to be drawn showing the accumulative flying hours per aircraft, so that one could see at a glance if too many of them were heading for minor and major inspections at one time. With that all resolved, we began to fly in earnest. It was the first time the flight commanders could each lead their full complement of six Spitfires into the air, and the orders were to practise quasi-combat flying and to tidy up display formation flying. Pairs of aircraft were also flown so that pilots could use their cine-cameras against their partner flying straight and level, also in dogfights. Needless to say, their films were evaluated with great care, and those who were not up to the mark were given ground instruction and intensive marksmanship practice in the air.

When the pilots were ready, I took them up on squadron formation flights, starting them off with conventional formations; sections of four Spitfires, three flying in vic with one in the box behind the leader. (A vic formation of three aircraft is elementary, consisting of the leader with one aircraft flying slightly behind his wing on the starboard and another to his port. If a fourth flies in line astern of the leader, he is the man in the box because that aircraft makes up a box formation.) Two sections would fly on my wings. From there we practised battle formation by flying sections in finger four, each section widely separated from me on either side, making a frontage of a mile or so. The Germans used this formation in 1940 with devastating effect, while we put our lives at risk by flying close Hendon formations.

When the pilots were effective, I would rotate the lead position between the flight commanders and their deputies. Sometimes I took off before the squadron, gained a 10,000 feet altitude advantage, and attacked them out of the sun. On my first attack I 'shot down' half the squadron, but they gradually learned the counter-moves.

Then I played silly buggers and flew peacetime formations which none of the pilots had attempted before. We flew twelve aircraft in line abreast formation, wing tip to wing tip. There is always a slight wobble with aircraft in formation which increased dramatically along the line of Spitfires, so that those on the outside were rising and falling ten feet above and below me, but ground observers would not have noticed this. I hardly dared make a turn of more than a half a degree in this formation as it was possible for aircraft to slide into the turn and collide with each other. Physically it was extremely hard work for the pilots on the outside to cope with, so I didn't keep it up for long. Twelve aircraft in line astern was also tricky, and if the pilot directly behind me skidded a little it caused a kind of shock wave which resulted in the arse end charlie skidding thirty feet out of line. Aircraft were stepped down along the line to avoid the slip-stream effects from those ahead. It needed thirteen Spitfires to fly the arrow formation, six on each side echeloned back from me. This is the way formations of wild geese fly, and seen from the ground it is impressive.

CHAPTER 15

While I was honing the cutting edge of No 1 squadron, I was also pulling strings to get it redeployed to its home base, Tangmere. I prepared the ground by writing to officers who had either commanded it or been flight commanders before the war, and who had by now risen in rank and power. When Japan capitulated, I increased my lobby and all were in agreement that the squadron must return to its mother base. There is not much point in farting against thunder, and HQ Fighter Command was busy as the devil accepting squadrons from Germany and finding airfields to place them on. The Air Ministry was deciding which squadrons to maintain in the front line and which to disband, for the overall strength was far greater than the peacetime requirement. They made some heinous errors of judgement. They should have retained the more senior squadrons and those which had gained fame in the World Wars; they did so in the case of No 617 (Dambuster) squadron in Bomber Command. But as to Fighter Command, it seemed that they stuck a pin along a list of numbers, and where the pin landed that number was to be retained in the front line. They even disbanded No 43 squadron, the pride of Fighter Command before the war (not that had it been idle during the war). They dared not, of course, disband the senior squadron in the RAF, which would have been tantamount to the pre-war Navy scuttling *HMS Hood*!

The AOC 12 Group had been promoted to an influential post in the Air Ministry, and when the seed bed had been nicely laid, I sent him a signal:

'Some months ago you instructed me to turn No 1 Squadron into an operational unit. This instruction has been successfully implemented. I have exhausted possibilities at Hutton Cranswick and suggest the squadron should be returned to its home base, Tangmere, to lead the way. *In omnibus princeps.*' (There's got to be a first time for everything, which was the squadron motto.)

My lobbyists had obviously been leaning on him for I received a signal by return.

'No 1 squadron is to redeploy to Tangmere as soon as maybe. Lead kindly light.'

The Adjutant booked a room in the nearest large pub for that evening and the whole squadron complement set off in cars and lorries. The formula was that I would pay half, the officers would pay pro rata according to rank for free drinks for the Corporals and airmen; the SNCOs could make their own arrangements, but no hard drinks were to be served. It cost me a small fortune. Before they started to fall over, I congratulated them on their hard work in difficult circumstances and said I wanted one extra effort from them. On the morrow, the maintenance crews were to make every attempt to finish off aircraft on inspections to have them ready to fly the following day. Crews on the line, assisted by the officers, were to clean and polish the Spitfires. There were gurgles of protest, but I intervened and told them that they could then pack their bags because I was getting them out of this hell-hole and taking them to Sussex by the sea. The volume of beer consumed intensified as they discussed the matter.

The next day I had ten balls in the air at one time. A small advance party under an officer and an SNCO was sent off in a coach with their own and the pilots' small kit. Their job was to sort the accommodation reserved in the officers and sergeants messes and the airmen's barrack block at Tangmere. A special train had to be laid on with covered wagons for the main party, consisting of the bulk of the NCOs and men, the heavy luggage of all personnel, spare parts for the aircraft and so on. Heavy items such as cranes and starter batteries were left behind, and spares were superficially accounted for. The LNER were surprisingly efficient, and a passenger-cum-goods train was soon in position at the nearest railhead where lorries plied to and fro for most of the day. Guards armed with rifles, but no ammunition, were detailed to keep watch over the train overnight. Meanwhile, a gang of men under the eagle eye of Dusty Miller, were cleaning out the billets, leaving everything as shipshape as possible. The maintenance crews, reinforced by line crews, worked long into the night, and they managed to get the full complement of sixteen Spitfires on the line.

I told the railway authorities to hitch on a locomotive and get steam up, then we took off, whereupon the ground crews drove in convoy to the train. It was a calm clear day and we flew at 400 mph, at 2,000 feet, on course for Tangmere. One of my pin-points was the house where my wife was staying with her mother, which was slap on course, and as we closed range I ordered the squadron into tight formation, went into a dive and opened my throttle. We passed over the house at 400 feet, meaning that the arse end charlies who were stepped down were at 200 feet. The cows grazing on her cousin's adjoining land gave sour milk for a fortnight. We overflew the Thames and the Sussex Downs loomed on the horizon. In close formation we cleared the hills and dived at Tangmere, my target being Station Headquarters. The arse end charlies all but took the flag-pole down, then I hauled back into a steep climb and vanished from sight over the sea beyond Bognor. I rang up the Tower and asked what runway was in use, put the squadron into aircraft echelon starboard, sections line astern and descended low and fast over the up-wind runway. When I cleared it I ordered the squadron to break for landing. I hauled back in a tight climbing turn to port with my number two on my wing, and the rest of the squadron did likewise at five second intervals. Thus there were eight pairs of Spitfires flying throttled back on the down-wind leg of the runway. At the end of the leg, I slapped the undercart down, made a tight gliding turn on the approach, and gave her full flaps. I deliberately landed almost half-way up the runway to allow room for the rest.

As I turned off the runway, I saw all sixteen aircraft on the runway at one time, which was pretty slick work.

I taxied to the dispersal area and swung the Spitfire onto the grass facing into wind, and the pilots formed neat line abreast formation before they shut down their engines. One of the advance party helped me get unstrapped, and I jumped off the wing only to be confronted by a tall officer wearing a scowl. He had half a stripe more on his uniform than I did, which made him a Wing Commander who was also the Station Commander.

'What the bloody hell do you think you're doing, trying to knock my flag-pole down!' he screeched.

I removed my flying helmet.

'If I had tried to knock your flag-pole down, Sir,' I reasoned, 'you wouldn't now have a flag-pole. Anyway, this squadron has the freedom of Tangmere.'

'It bloody well hasn't any longer,' he informed me. 'From now on you do what I bloody well tell you!'

'Come, come, Sir,' I said soothingly. 'Long time no see. I was on 66 squadron in 1940 and you were with 19 squadron at Duxford.'

'Dizzy!' he exclaimed. 'God help me! I knew that No 1 squadron was flying in, but nobody told me you were in command. If I'd known, I'd have stopped the move.'

'You'd have been bloody lucky,' I said. 'No one could have stopped the move except God.'

He was Wilfred Clouston, a tall tough New Zealander, wearing a black moustache. He was a strict disciplinarian, something of a martinet, and I don't normally care for people who throw their weight around unnecessarily. However, leadership comes in many moods, and whereas Wilfred may not have been generally liked, he was respected. He certainly had the sense to ride me on a loose rein, which is the way I prefer. Furthermore, I was the senior Squadron Leader on the Station, which made me deputy Station Commander, and if he wanted to take leave, or went sick or anything, he automatically handed his command over to me. This made for a close relationship, and we also shared our Duxford experiences; there were mighty few ex-Duxford pilots, 1940 vintage, still breathing by now. We got along fine, and if he occasionally wanted to bawl me out, I didn't mind, kept my mouth shut and waited for him to cool down. I said I'd have a look around and report to him formally the next morning, and then I did a quick inspection of the area for which I was responsible. It was pretty horrific. Wartime squadrons coming in and leaving had certainly taken their toll. Nothing positive could be done until the main party arrived, so after the officers and airmen had picketed the aircraft down I told them to shove off for the rest of the day.

CHAPTER 16

At 0830 hours the next day I marched into Wilfred's office, saluted and bade him good morning. He gestured me into a chair and asked me how I found things.

'I'm afraid my parish on the Station is suffering from war wounds,' I said. 'I propose to put my main effort into cleaning it up, and merely keep the flying side ticking over.'

'How long do you want?' he asked.

'We'll be flat out for a fortnight,' I estimated, 'then we can relax a bit. It won't be straight for a month. I also want to make some structural alterations to the squadron dispersal huts.'

'Such as?'

'My office is too small to swing a cat, certainly not big

85

enough to have an airman on a charge marched in. Similarly with the squadron stores, and my Flight Sergeants haven't got their own offices to keep the aircraft maintenance schedules and the rest in. They can't bawl an airman out in privacy. I want to remove those poisonous coke stoves from the pilots' room, same with the airmen's rest room, and replace them with portable electric radiators. The huts will have to be rewired and painted, and God knows what.'

'Don't forget I've got to run this Station on a strict budget,' he muttered uneasily. 'There are more units on this Station than just your squadron.'

'Not to my mind,' I replied. 'In any case, not to worry. I know all the works people round here. I'll get it done on the cheap. It might cost me a few bottles of whisky though. No doubt you will authorize payment from the airmen's welfare fund?'

'Like bloody hell I won't,' he snarled. 'That would be highly irregular.'

'On your head be it, Sir,' I murmured. 'Arthur King who runs the Unicorn would give me a case for free. I'd make an occasion of it and call a press conference, with photographers taking pictures of him handing me a case of whisky with the squadron aircraft as a background. I can see the headlines in the *Chichester Gazette* now: PUBLICAN RESCUES SENIOR SQUADRON IN THE RAF. IS THE STATION COMMANDER AS PARSIMONIOUS AS HE LOOKS.'

'Are you bloody mad!' he shrieked.

'You should know, Sir.'

'No doubt some compromise can be arranged,' he fumed. 'Now I've got one for you. I want you to take on the job as President of the Mess Committee.'

'Eh?' I stuttered. 'What me? I'll have my work cut out licking things into shape on my own account.'

'All right,' he replied. 'You can take over as PMC in a month's time. I want to get the Mess back into pre-war demeanour. You and I are the only pre-war officers on the Station.'

'OK, Sir, I'll do it, but only for three months. Then my wife will be taking on a married quarter, and you can't have a living out officer as PMC.'

We parted quite amicably.

The main party arrived at the goods railhead at Chichester, and the rest of the day was spent ferrying stores from there to the dispersal and the hangar – yes, we had our own hangar for a change. We checked that we had our quota of cranes, jacks, motor transport and so on, and sufficient starter batteries were hauled by tractors to the dispersal. Dusty Miller allocated various dormitories to the airmen and their heavy baggage was dumped in the barracks, similarly with the sergeants' and officers'. When everything was reasonably shipshape, personnel were released from duty to sort themselves out. For those without cars, there was a decent bus service to Chichester. People with cars had been authorized to drive down from Yorkshire, but those pilots detailed to fly got somebody else to drive theirs for them.

Then I went to see the Clerk of Works, who eyed me suspiciously.

'I thought you'd be along to see me,' he grunted. 'How can I help?'

'Nothing much, Jack,' I said. 'No need to make notes, I've got a list. Here you are.'

He read it and his eyes boggled.

'Pull down partition walls. Rewire buildings. Remove coke stoves. Fashion new offices. Make good and repaint barrack block. Goddamn it, Sir! If I put all my men onto this, it would take a fortnight.'

'That's what I thought, Jack. A fortnight will do fine.'

87

'But the bloody Station Commander wants the Guard Room redecorated, the Officers Mess painted, a new bath put in his bloody residence and the Lord knows what else. I'm going mad!'

'No need, Jack. He wants you to give priority to my requirements.'

'Did he say that in so many words?' he enquired suspiciously.

'I can't remember what he said, but that was the gist of it. If he brings it up, be tactful. Say that your men are on strike or something. In any case, my men will give you a hand. I'll put a gang under your foreman, and my electricians can help with the wiring. More than that, we will paint the inside and outside of the huts ourselves if you provide the paint and brushes.'

'That would certainly help, but I can't do it in a fortnight.'

'As a matter of fact, I'm letting you off lightly. It's really your job to clean the parquet floors in the barrack block with your electric sanding device. There is five years of grime embedded in those floors. But if you lend me your sander and three electric polishers, we'll do it ourselves. Incidentally, I seem to remember that you enjoyed a tot of whisky now and again.'

His eyes lit up.

'I'd go bloody mad without my whisky of an evening,' he informed me.

'Well, I'll give you a bottle tomorrow, another in a week's time, and provided you've done a good job, a third at the end of it. You've got to start tomorrow to qualify, mark you.'

'Done!' he said. 'Bugger the Station Commander's bath.'

'That's the spirit Jack! Whisky I mean.'

My next port of call was on the Barrack Warden, whose

office was in a large repository filled with furniture of every kind, even down to pre-war bed-pots.

'Bill,' I said, 'there's been a nasty accident. We piled out all the furniture in my dispersal huts to clean it, then some silly bugger set light to the pile. I want new furniture and curtains.'

'I thought something like that would happen,' he snarled. 'The Clerk of Works tipped me off that you were on the prowl. How much whisky are you going to give me?'

'Two bottles,' I told him, 'provided you let me have half a dozen portable electric radiators.'

'I don't stock them,' he informed me.

'All right. Three bottles or I'll declare the squadron non-operational. It's cold enough at 40,000 feet, but I can't have my pilots and ground crews frozen on the ground. Buy them with a local purchase order.'

With that achieved we could now make a start. We laid on a strictly limited flying programme, mainly navigation flights to familiarize the pilots with the territory covered by HQ 11 Group, which ranged from Land's End to mid-Wales and across to Suffolk. Particular note had to be made of prominent landmarks, in case of poor visibility, and I emphasized the importance of the Arundel Gap. Whereas the Sussex Downs reach up to about 800 feet, the valley of the Arun River forms a gap in the Downs which falls to sea-level by the town of Arundel. The Gap had saved my life on several occasions. At this time we had no ground based airfield radar aids, although the radar chain proper could home us back over the airfield. We adopted a 'QGH' procedure, whereby radar would home us above the airfield at 20,000 feet when the ground was obscured by thick cloud. If the cloud lowered to ground level, there was no point in attempting to land and all one could do was to divert to another airfield where cloud base was more reasonable, or bale out. Unlike larger aircraft the Spitfire carried precious little fuel for much of a diversion, which is why I kept my eye on the weather like a hawk in search of prey. The weather pattern can change with great rapidity, and although I listened patiently to the met forecasters, whose synoptic charts did come in handy, more often than not I made my own predictions. Quite often the forecasters would proclaim that it was not fit to fly, but if I disagreed with them I would take off on a weather recce and ring up the Tower to tell the Flight Commanders whether or not to fly. One day a met officer was telling my pilots that it would be a bright blue day, but I was looking out of the window. When he had finished his briefing, I asked him why it was snowing.

All I had to do was to look out of the window. It is the type of cloud and its formation which portends the weather prospects, and these are changing every minute. I could easily diagnose whether a warm, cold, or occluded front was on the way, when fog was a possibility, or on a blue hot day whether there would be an inversion at 5,000 feet keeping industrial haze gathered below that point, which would bring slant visibility down to half a mile. During the whole of my RAF career the aircraft I flew were far more sophisticated than the landing aids. Admittedly, I got to the stage when I had a licence to take off and land jets such as the Canberra bomber with a cloud base of 100 feet and visibility half a mile. Even so, I was entirely reliant on my R/T set remaining serviceable. Oddly enough, no one thought about fitting two R/T sets in case one blew up!

However, having passed overhead at 20,000 feet, I would ask the controller to clear me for a QGH approach. He would rely on his antiquated, time-consuming radio loops in an attempt to maintain a bearing on the aircraft. I would commence my descent heading over the sea, and he would put a stop-watch on me. At 10,000 feet he would direct me to turn on such and such a heading, maintaining my rate of descent. In theory, this would set me on course for the airfield, but in fact wind drift might cock that all up. Hopefully, I would break cloud at, say, 1,000 feet in sight of the coast, and make my way back visually.

CHAPTER 17

We could keep the limited amount of flying ticking over with comparatively few men, and the rest were detailed into gangs. I told Dusty Miller to pick up the sander and the polishers from the Clerk of Works and set his gang to work on the barrack block, also to cajole the foreman into getting a move on. The pilots were to paint the outside of their hut while adjustments were being made to the internal accommodation, and the airmen painted their hut and the stores building. But the most appalling prospect was the area behind the buildings. Wartime squadrons came and went, and to put it mildly they didn't give a damn about the mess they left behind. In an area the size of a couple of tennis courts, covered with lanky weeds and couch grass, was the debris of war, a positive junk heap. There were fifty gallon oil drums, some still full of oil, hulks of motor cars, jerry cans with petrol in them, old newspapers, broken china, tin cans – you name it, it was there. Apart from the fact that it was an unhygienic eyesore, it was also a marvellous fire risk. To dispose of this entailed the use of cranes, and lorries making constant journeys to and from the Council tip. The fire brigade had an old airframe on a derelict part of the Station which they set light to regularly to see how soon they could put out the blaze, and they were only too pleased to remove the inflammable material.

It is amazing at what a couple of hundred men can achieve if they have the will and supervision. Easily within a month, the buildings under my aegis were in pristine condition – if one can apply the word pristine to wooden shacks, a hangar and a barrack block. Then, I could lay the foundations for further progress. Each officer was given a secondary duty, for example being in charge of the airmen's welfare, athletics, rugby, soccer or cricket. I introduced the officer i/c gardens and his deputy to Job, the head groundsman.

'These chaps know sweet fanny adams about gardens,' I said.

'What's that got to do with me? I'm in charge of the playing fields, the Officers Mess garden, the gardens belonging to the Station proper, and cutting the grass on the airfield. That's all.'

'What about the cricket pitch? We're forming a team and I bowl slow off-spin with the odd chinaman. Rough it up a bit near the stumps.'

'Me rough up the pitch for you! Not bloody likely.'

'You don't enjoy looking at the Mess outside my dispersal huts, Job, do you?'

'I think it's a bloody disgrace.'

'That makes two of us. Come and have a look.'

I drove him to the dispersal.

'I thought a few rose-beds would be enough to give it a bit of colour,' I said.

'Yes, that would be enough. I'll mark them out when you've cut the grass; it's as high as my head.'

'I want you to cut the grass, Job. None of my chaps can use a scythe, and after that it will need to be cut properly. Lend me a couple of men for a day or two.'

'I can't spare any men. Anyway, what's in it for me?'

'Two bottles of whisky,' I replied.

'You gave the bloody Clerk of Works and the Barrack Warden three bottles each,' he announced.

'Oh! Did I? It slipped my memory. OK, I'll make it three on condition that you provide the best roses for the purpose.'

'All right,' he grumbled. 'And I'll put them in for you.'

All that was needed after that was a large notice board and a sign-writer. He inscribed on the board: 'No 1 (Fighter) Squadron—In omnibus princeps.' Then we could fly.

It isn't difficult to make a figure '1' in the sky with aircraft. All it needed was to echelon an aircraft port on my wing, put seven aircraft into line astern on me, with two more in line abreast on the arse end charlie. When we had tamed the technique, we regularly overflew Chichester at 1,000 feet to remind the citizens of our presence at nearby Tangmere. We also flew our fancy formations, and practised gunnery and tactics using cine-cameras. To exercise the guns and the armourers we fired at ground targets on a gunnery range at Chesil Beach, west of Weymouth. I objected to the use of this range, but it was the only one available. In the first place, there was a famous swannery behind the beach right on our line of approach low at the targets. Understandably enough, the swans became extremely agitated as we overflew their nests at about 400 feet. Next, the beach consisted of pebbles, and there was every possibility that ricocheting cannon shell could endanger the aircraft that was firing. I spelt this out in a signal to 11 Group, but our superiors pooh-poohed my objections. I warned the pilots, which didn't do much good for they would have to get close enough to the targets to hit them.

However, the thing was solved once and for all when I observed a Spitfire taxiing in trickling white smoke. As he

93

stopped his engine, I yelled at the pilot to get out of the cockpit pronto, having first alerted the fire brigade. We kept a safe distance away to give the engine time to cool down, then I climbed on the wing and noted that the glycol temperature was much too high. The pilot told me that the temperature had begun to rise on the approach to the runway, and I told him he was a silly bugger for not switching the engine off while on the runway. On inspection, the coolant system was all but dry, and there were several holes in the radiator. There was no question of pilot error, as the Range Safety Officer confirmed. The pilot, John Vidals, had made a perfectly normal attack and had holed the target. His break away had commenced no lower than usual, but he had been struck by rebounding cannon shell or pebbles.

I sent an immediate signal to 11 Group, with copies to HQFC and the Air Ministry. This was one of my favourite gimmicks when I wanted something done in haste. I invariably was hauled over the coals by Group HQ for going above their heads to HQFC and the Air Ministry, to which my standard reply would be that I was merely keeping higher authority informed, leaving Group to take the executive action. In fact, as I very well knew, higher authority would breath down Group's neck, demanding to know what the bloody hell they were doing about it. To add to the agony, I marked the signal AIRCRAFT SAFETY, which always created a riot, and the message read: 'Despite previous warnings one of my aircraft was almost written off today through flying debris when using the Chesil Beach range. Request this range be declared non-operational with immediate effect. Also that the King be informed that breeding in the nearby swannery is being jeopardized by constant overflight of aircraft at low level. You will be aware that swans come under the Royal prerogative.'

94

That fixed it! An immediate signal to all fighter stations was despatched to HQFC within a few hours. 'Chesil Beach firing range is disbanded forthwith. All range equipment to be withdrawn.' I hope the swans appreciated my endeavours.

When I had settled in, Wilfred Clouston decided to take some leave. He was one of those chaps who thought he was indispensable, whereas RAF policy lays it down that an officer's deputy should be capable of stepping into his shoes at a moment's notice. I was only too pleased to delegate my duties, although I quite often had to clean up the mess on my return. The fact that Wilfred had held his commission for three years longer than myself was of little consequence – I too had commanded stations, albeit not of such importance as Tangmere. He briefed me on every intricate detail of the Station, to which I listened with half an ear. He had decided to take a fortnight's leave, and I suggested he made it a month. He gazed at me suspiciously, and his eyes asked the unspoken question – could I hold down the job for that length of time without making a balls up? I conned him by telling him certain aspects of the Station he had never heard of, promising to keep an eye on those – which is more than he'd ever done! He tried to squeeze from me the promise that I would hand over No 1 squadron to my senior flight commander, and spend all my time supervising the Station, but I deflected this. He was going to Nice, and I swore that if things became too much for me I would send down a clapped-out Anson to Nice airport to bring him back before I hanged myself in his office.

In fact, I changed my routine very little. I would go to his office and read the mail, draft replies where necessary, and generally let the Station Adjutant get on with things, but I did perform the Station Commander's Saturday inspections of the camp as a whole. There were only two incidents worthy of note. An airman committed a felony serious enough to warrant a Court Martial, which is a time-consuming and expensive business. I rang up the personnel people at Group and told them that assuming I found him guilty, I reckoned my maximum powers of punishment would about suit the case; if not, they would have to convene a Court Martial. They said that I should for God's sake avoid the pother of a CM if possible. I found him guilty, and in such cases Air Force Law demands that the accused should be asked if he would accept summary punishment, or prefer to go before a CM. When asked, he said he would prefer a CM, blast him. I adjourned the case to allow him to cool down and had him in again, pointing out that whereas my powers of punishment were limited, those of a CM were not. Furthermore, I had found him guilty and he had no witnesses for his defence, so there was every likelihood that a CM would also find him guilty. In which case, he would be roughed up in a detention centre, whereas under summary punishment he would be stuck in jug at Tangmere. I assured him that Tangmere was soft stuff compared with a military prison such as Colchester. He used his loaf and said he would accept my punishment, whereupon I slapped him behind bars at Tangmere for fifty-six days. Sure, he had to polish the Guard Room floor etcetera every day, but that was his fault for committing a crime. Summary justice is not rough justice.

Much worse than that, I was told that Geoffrey de Havilland's son would be flying the prototype of a new fighter to Tangmere in an attempt to beat the world high speed record. Mine not to reason why, but my hair curled at the prospect of using a prototype for this purpose. The idea was that observers with measuring equipment would base themselves at Tangmere and proceed to their various vantage posts when the aircraft flew the course at top

Horse power from Sussex shire-horses, 1940 *(courtesy South Eastern Newspapers Ltd)*

Author's Spitfire shot down by British ack-ack, 1940

Quicker by rail – one Tangmere Hurricane written off, 1940 *(courtesy Imperial War Museum)*

Battle-damaged Spitfire, Tangmere 1940 *(courtesy Imperial War Museum)*

Author's Lagonda in war-time trim, Tangmere 1943

Author piloting Spitfire Mk XXI Contraprop, Tangmere 1947

Squadron, flight commanders and a few pilots, Tangmere 1950

After the ball was over – Tangmere 1950

OPPOSITE ABOVE: Turning port, aircraft echeloned starboard – 43 squadron's Meteors Mk VIII, Tangmere 1951

OPPOSITE BELOW: The author in action post-war – farewell theatricals at Tangmere, 1951

The beautiful lines of the Hunter. 43 squadron was the first to re-equip with them

speed over the sea. The pilot would land at Tangmere and the aircraft would be serviced by fitters from the de Havilland Aircraft Company. My role was to ensure that any facilities we could give them were made available. The C-in-C Fighter Command rang me up and told me to ensure that we did all we could to assist and to give them decent food. My immediate reaction was that if he wanted above average food I would make them pay through the nose for it.

It was a non-event. Shortly before the trials were due, the pilot was killed in his prototype aircraft. Tragically, he was the second of Sir Geoffrey's sons to suffer that fate in Company aircraft.

When Wilfred returned to his office I was waiting for him, sitting in his chair with my feet on the desk. I arose and asked him if he had enjoyed his holiday, which query he brushed aside.

'Anything happened while I was away?' he demanded to know.

'Nothing much, Sir,' I said calmly. 'Oh, one of the hangars was destroyed by fire, but there was nothing we could do about that. We pranged ten aircraft, which was an act of God I'm afraid. And you'd better go to sick quarters for a jab. There's an epidemic of typhoid here. The filters in the water tower were invaded by rats.'

For a moment he almost believed me, then he noticed my grin.

'Dammit,' he said disappointedly. 'Do you mean to say *nothing* untoward happened?'

'Why should it? Any bloody fool can run a station.'

CHAPTER 18

Ideally, if you delegate your responsibilities you should hand them over to someone you can trust. On the other hand, as I intended to take a fortnight's leave, I had to delegate command of the squadron to my senior flight commander. He was the guy I had to rehabilitate at Hutton Cranswick, and whereas he was all right in the air, he was unsound on the ground. He had no instinct for man management and, although under military discipline, NCOs and airmen can be a prickly lot if they are not handled properly and resentment is a difficult emotion to quell. I returned from leave quite late at night and had gone to my room to sort things out and drink a little whisky, when there was a knock on the door. I yelled at whoever it was to come in, the door opened and lo and behold! it was Dusty Miller, still in uniform. He had a chin like a boot, protruding ears, a fierce glare or a wide grin which exposed his gleaming white dentures depending on his mood. He was always slightly hollow-cheeked, but he now looked positively gaunt.

'Come in, Dusty,' I said. 'Take a chair and have a drop of mother's milk. What the hell do you want?'

'Highly irregular entering an officer's room, Sir,' he said, 'but I've got some bad news.'

'That can wait. Sit down and have some whisky.' I poured him half a tumbler, neat.

He removed his cap and sat in an arm chair looking at the whisky appreciatively. 'I've already had half a bottle,' he announced, 'but this will do no harm. You, Sir, have got a mutiny on your hands!'

Among his many roles, Dusty was what you might call

my Head of KGB. He kept his nose to the ground regarding airmen's grievances and so on and gave me early warning.

Whisky spluttered from my mouth at the news and I poured myself a tougher mix.

'What the bloody hell are you talking about?' I expostulated. 'What mutiny?'

Before he finished his narrative, another half tumbler had gone down his gullet.

It appeared that Fighter Command had to indulge in a massive fly-past over London in about a month's time to celebrate victory over Germany and Japan. This would be the precursor to an almighty parade comprising regiments from all elements in the British, Commonwealth and Empire countries. However, airmen were now being demobbed in stages, and those coming up for demobilization were counting the calendars. Their hopes had been shattered by a new order to the effect that those due for demob were now to wait until the fly-past was over and done with, to ensure that sufficient aircraft were available for the task. My flight commander had informed the men of this in an off-hand manner, without a full explanation. Resentment had now reached boiling point, and Dusty judged that small pockets of mutineers would display their feelings in a way which would land them into trouble.

'OK, Dusty,' I said. 'Alert the Adjutant that I want a full parade of all airmen and officers at 0830 hours tomorrow.'

When they were paraded, I arrived with a soap box and stood on it. I told the ranks the reason why, pointing out that this V Day parade in London was part of a form of thanksgiving, and the salute would be taken by the King and Queen together with Winston Churchill. Troops from every quarter of the globe were already being shipped over, the Navy would be doing its stuff in its own way, and it was an honour for Fighter Command to represent the RAF as a whole. No 1 squadron would have the leading role, and if they had any pride in the squadron, then they should show it. Those due for demob shortly were the ones who had put in the longest war service, and when they came to think about it what was another month in the RAF after five years. I ended by saying that if any of them felt aggrieved at being kept back from Civvy Street, then they should apply to Flight Sergeant Miller who would march them in to see me. Those with genuine compassionate reasons would receive a sympathetic hearing.

Surprisingly enough, only a dozen wanted to see me. Mark it, Dusty had put others through the mesh, and those whose grandmothers were on their deathbeds – when they weren't – had been told to bugger off and not waste my time. Of the remainder, an airman's wife was about to have a baby in Cumbria, and he had a doctor's chit to prove it. He was given compassionate leave, which he would have received in any case. Another had been given a job at a garage at Portsmouth provided he could start work immediately after his discharge which was in a week's time. I rang up the manager explaining the position, and he promised to keep the job open until the man was formally discharged a few weeks later; so he stayed. About half of them had genuine cases for immediate release, and they were sent on leave with instructions to report back to be officially demobilized on the due date. The rest were sent back to normal duties, satisfied at least that they had been given a fair hearing.

A few days later I bumped into Dusty Miller and enquired as to whatever happened to his mutiny.

'I'll have ye know, Sir, that a mutiny was brewing up all right, but you deflated it. The trouble was that your flight commander didn't keep the men informed, still less attempt to listen to some genuine grievances. Begging

100

your pardon, but he didn't show the necessary qualities of leadership.'

The operation order for the V Day fly-past arrived and I studied it. It was a pig's breakfast, demanding tens of squadrons to fly in parade formation up the Mall heading for Buckingham Palace. To fly up the Mall meant an approach along the Thames from east to west, and I reckoned that the formation leaders would follow the curves of the Thames, not in a straight line for the saluting base which would be positioned half way up the Mall. This would put the tail end charlies into a flat spin as they skidded from side to side. I wondered whether the squadrons had bothered to practise parade formations as we had done; if not half a dozen mid-air collisions could be expected. To cap it all, there was no bad weather plan – formation leaders were to fly at 1,500 feet with the trailing sections flying slightly below. This presupposed that there would be a cloud base of 2,000 feet with good visibility to allow formations from various stations to join up near the mouth of the Thames. The Staff seemed to expect perfect June weather, neglecting the fact that Eisenhower's D Day amphibious vessels were all but shipwrecked in June, and at about the same time of year the Spanish Armada was indeed shipwrecked. I hoped the mid-air collisions would not drop on the saluting base.

But we were out of this mêlée. Since we had the fastest aircraft in Fighter Command, with a service ceiling far above that of the other squadrons, our task was to lay contrails high in the sky to herald the approach of the mass formations. The trouble was that no one knew when contrails formed and why. In the war they were a definite menace for they could be seen by the enemy miles away, and he could easily jump the formation that was creating them. If we started to smoke, the arse end charlies would say so, and the leader could either attempt a quick climb in the hope of clearing the contrail area, or he would fly below it. Broadly speaking, contrails are formed by the heat of exhaust stubs condensing clear, humid air at height. They might issue as mere whisps fifty feet long, or they might extend for miles and remain for up to half an hour. However, even when winds at ground level are slack, they might be blowing at 150 mph at great height, in which case long contrails are almost immediately dispersed by wind forces. Pressure trails can sprout from the wing tips of a fighter performing a high gee turn at low level in conditions of high humidity, but these are something different. Of course, in 1946 we relied on our red-hot exhausts for the heat necessary to form contrails, a far cry from the jet age when air is thrust from the engine effluxes at temperatures of 2,000 degrees Celsius. To put it mildly, the Staff was baying at the moon.

No matter, I decided to accumulate all possible data involving the formation of contrails. Every day we would consult with the met officers in an attempt to elucidate conditions of sudden humidity at great height, which to them was unexplored territory. The Met Office, then based at Dunstable, took an interest but they were of little help. The only readings the met boys could give us depended on measuring equipment attached to quite large balloons filled with hydrogen gas, but all that could be gleaned from those amounted to the speed of the jet-stream, if any, at 40,000 feet. So aircraft took off in pairs several times a day, and the pilots had scribbling pads strapped to their thigh to take notes. If the leader's Spitfire began to make smoke, his number two would inform him and jot down the exact height when the contrails appeared, what sort of contrails they were, and the leader would continue to climb to see if he could get out of the contrail area. When I was in the lead with a contraprop, my number two in a five blader, I would give her full throttle at 30,000 feet and soar away from him to 45,000 feet, but he could still keep me in sight. The data we gained was fed to the Met Office, but it didn't seem to help them in elucidating the conditions of the air at height.

After a fortnight's trials I rang up the Group Captain in charge of Operations at 11 Group.

'I can't guarantee to produce contrails for the V Day flypast,' I told him.

'But you've got to,' he replied with enormous asininity.

Patience is not my strong point, but I decided to fill him in. I explained that we had been continuing trials for a fortnight, and on only a quarter of the sorties flown did we make thick contrails of the required type. However, on half those occasions the strong winds dispersed them almost immediately. Therefore there was a ten per cent chance of producing contrails on V Day, but he had better halve that because there was no point in making smoke if the sky was obscured by cloud.

'I don't believe you,' he stuttered. 'In the Battle of Britain, they kept making contrails. I know, I've seen photographs of them.'

'Any sod with any tactical nous avoided the contrail layer. What were you in 1940 anyhow – a bloody Air Raid Warden?'

'You can't talk to me like that, I'm a Senior officer in charge of . . .'

'Sorry,' I replied. 'I thought you were a fucking Pilot Officer – you sound like one.'

CHAPTER 19

On the eve of V Day I looked at the clouds and decided that an occluded front was slowly approaching London from the west, and that the existing low clouds with drizzle would continue for several days. The met synoptic charts merely confirmed my opinion, so did the met officer. Early next morning the situation was unchanged, and the charts showed the front almost stationary over London. The cloud base was tending to lower and visibility in the drizzle was poor. There was not the slightest prospect of laying on a fly-past over London or anywhere else south of the Wash. I waited until the Staff officers staggered into their offices and rang up the chap in charge of Ops.

'I'm putting my aircraft to bed for the day,' I informed him. 'You'll not get any contrails out of me, and if I made them no one would see them from the ground. Furthermore, I hope you have cancelled the fly-past else you'll prang half of Fighter Command's aircraft.'

'Don't be silly,' he said. 'The clouds might break up in time.'

'They bloody well won't. Have you looked at the met charts?'

'No. I've only just arrived in my office. In any case, I don't understand met charts with all their squiggles.'

'There are a lot of things you don't understand,' I said. 'But I've written a note to be opened on my death. In it I state that anyone who allows this fly-past to take off should be court martialled and shot.'

'Oh do be a sport,' he babbled. 'I can't stop this fly-past. The King will be there.'

'In which case His Majesty will get bloody wet,' I said. 'Ring up the Palace and tell him to wear a raincoat.'

'I insist that you take off on time,' he cried. 'Do stop bullying me, I don't feel well.'

'I reckon you'll be dead before the day's out,' I warned him unsympathetically.

I briefed the squadron. Cloud base was at about 600 feet and I would level out at 400 feet with my section in line astern formation, slowly orbiting the airfield to allow the other sections to form up on me. 'A' flight commander's section would form up on my right wing, aircraft in line astern but slightly echeloned to starboard to avoid the arse end charlies snaking into each other. 'B' flight commander's section would do likewise on my port wing. A spare pilot would follow and when he reported twelve Spitfires in position, he was to return to base and land. I would then fly out to sea, make a gentle turn heading for Tangmere, opening my throttle to climbing revs as I did so, and commence my ascent on course for Canterbury. When in cloud, flight commanders were to maintain close formation on me, but if cloud conditions were so thick that they lost sight of me, they were to turn on a heading five degrees from my course, maintain their rate of climb, and intercept me with the help of radar above cloud. I pointed out, however, that I believed I would still be in cloud at 30,000 feet, in which case I would abort the mission.

The cloud was certainly thick, but fortunately not turbulent as we proceeded steadily on the climb. Even in close formation, wisps of cloud obscured the flight commanders and my Spitfire, and I suggested they break on a separate course as briefed. Not a bit of it! They hung on for grim death. The fact of the matter was that their instrument flying was not accurate enough to proceed independently, so I was their only hope. I levelled off at

30,000 feet and the cloud was so black above that I reckoned it went up beyond 40,000 feet. I told the flight commanders I was returning to base and that they should stay in tight formation. I called up the radar station at Heathrow and asked for homing assistance back to Tangmere and a woman's voice replied. My nerves by this time were somewhat jaded from all out concentration on instruments.

'I don't want to talk to a bloody woman,' I said. 'Get me the controller.'

'I am the controller, Princeps leader,' she replied. 'Remember me?'

I remembered her all right! She was about the best radar controller in Fighter Command, and I knew her of old. She was a Squadron Officer in the WAAF.

'Yes, I remember you, duckie,' I said. 'Get me out of the shit, would you?'

She came over all professional and told me I was approaching Canterbury at angels 30. Would I turn to port, heading two three zero degrees. When I was on course I should commence my descent.

'Try and put me down over Arundel,' I told her. 'The Downs will be covered in cloud, but I can slip through the Arundel Gap.'

'Roger, Princeps leader. I'll feed into a GCI (Ground Control Interception) unit in that area. Keep your cool.'

'You sound like a bloody nanny,' I told her.

She kept altering my course to steer in general terms as we descended, but tightened up to precision controlling as we closed on the Downs, changing my course by just one degree port or starboard. She kept demanding that I should increase or decrease my rate of descent by a hundred feet a minute, and in due time by fifty feet a minute. I was hypnotized by the instrument flying panel as we neared the Downs, and sweat was pouring into my oxygen mask. The surrounding Down rose to 800 feet, so there was no room for error if twelve Spitfires were to avoid running into a stuffed cloud. I began to twitch when my altimeter indicated 800 feet, when she called up and said I was to continue my rate of descent, look ahead when I cleared cloud, when I would see Arundel ahead.

And my God! so it occurred.

I dropped down almost to sea-level, made a lazy turn to starboard and kept the coast in sight; but it was difficult to differentiate between the grey of the cloud and the grey of the sea, so I flew partly on instruments while snatching glances at the coast. Selsey Bill loomed out of the murk and I made a sharp turn to starboard, following the 'B' road leading to Chichester, and simultaneously ordered the squadron into landing formation. The two flight commanders throttled back and aircraft slid into echelon starboard formation on their leaders. I saw Chichester Cathedral ahead, and noted with interest that the weather vane was obscured in cloud. The spire is 270 feet high, so we had precious little room to spare. Modern airline pilots, despite their gadgetry, would not be allowed to land in such conditions. I told the Tower to switch on the runway lights to full brilliance, and informed the squadron I was making a final turn to land. The pilots slipped back into pairs and followed me down at 30 second intervals. I told them to lower their undercarts, then their flaps, and touched down some distance up the runway to allow them room to make their own landings. As I turned onto the taxi track, I noted that all the Spitfires were on the runway at the same time, proof positive of a slick landing in outrageous weather conditions. I taxied to the dispersal and climbed out to find Wilfred Clouston waiting for me. His neck was thick with throbbing veins, his face was puce and his dark eyes seemed to protrude from their sockets.

'May I ask what you think you are doing, taking a

squadron up when even the birds are walking?' he enquired with some asperity.

The relationship between a Station Commander and his senior squadron commander is always somewhat nebulous. In theory, he looked after the Station as a whole and left the airfield and the flying side of things to me. Nevertheless, if I had pranged any of my Spitfires – or all of them, which was eminently feasible in this case – the ultimate responsibility would fall on him.

'I thought it was a nice day to practise instrument flying,' I gaily replied.

'Don't give me that load of bullshit,' he snarled. 'The weather conditions are impossible, and you know it.'

'True, Sir. As a matter of fact I took off to placate the man in charge of Ops at 11 Group.'

'That old bugger! The last aeroplane he flew was a Hawker Hart, a bloody biplane.'

'I know. I used to enjoy flying the Hart. The screech of air through the rigging wires in a side-slip was music to my ears.'

'Would you kindly be serious. You should have told him to go to hell and stayed on the ground, or if necessary let me know so I could have told him to jump in the river.'

'I know. But he was in a bad way. But you've got another problem. As I was approaching Selsey, the Tower rang up and asked me to hold off because they had a Canadian squadron in difficulty. I couldn't hold off and barged in. They'll be here at any moment.'

He raced to my office, rang up the Tower and told them to divert the Canadians. The ATC boys informed him that no diversion bases were open: they were all weatherbound.

We watched the Canadians come in and they pranged four aircraft which missed the runway or undershot. Another overshot and turned port to make another attempt to land, which was orthodox procedure according to ATC patterns on the circuit. This was no place for orthodoxy, but some people get brainwashed into following the rules to the letter, a fault which I never suffered from. He should have turned starboard over the flat terrain which lays between Tangmere and Bognor. As it was, he hit a stuffed cloud half-way up the Goodwood Downs, and that was the end of him.

I rang up the Controller, Jane, and thanked her for her assistance.

'I haven't lost my touch,' she said demurely.

'Nor have I,' I told her. 'Come down here for a night and I'll give you a slap-up meal at Bosham.'

'If you haven't lost your touch,' she pronounced, 'the answer is not bloody likely. I don't want to be raped.'

'I wouldn't do a thing like that,' I protested.

'I'm not prepared to take the risk.'

Then I rang up Group Captain Ops, but his sidekick answered.

'How many aircraft did you prang?' I enquired.

'Oh Lord! We haven't counted them yet.'

'Well, add on another five which pranged at Tangmere. Where's the Group Captain?'

'He's been rushed to hospital with a heart attack.'

CHAPTER 20

For some time I had been holding down the job of PMC in my spare time. My main henchmen were Bill Barrell the Mess Secretary, Paddy the Senior Steward and major domo, Percy the senior chef, and Tom Griffiths the senior batman. Notionally, a meeting of Mess members was called every three months, but as Wilfred and I wanted to smarten up codes of Mess conduct, I held them every month. All officers not on essential duty had to attend or give their reasons in writing. The Mess was run on the lines of a London club, for the benefit of members in democratic style within the limits of Mess decorum. Thus members of the Committee were elected by a show of hands at a meeting, and they were stuck with the job for at least three months. Officers were voted in for various tasks. The wine chap had to account for the takings at the bar *vis-à-vis* the amount of drink consumed to ensure that the books were not being fiddled, also for the wine consumed at formal dinners. Officers would sign chits for their drinks – no money passed hands. The catering officer was supposed to supervise Percy and his cooks, which was a bit of a laugh because Percy knew it all. All he did was to accompany Percy and a few airmen in a lorry to the market, while Percy selected his own cuts of meat and so on. As Percy said to me, the art of cooking is in selecting the food. Percy could almost make a pâté from pigs' droppings, but in general the quality of food depended on how much the members were prepared to pay for it. The Air Ministry paid officers messes a ration for every living in officer which would barely have kept a tramp in sausages.

Then there was a house officer who would deal with complaints about dripping taps, cracks in ceilings, non-co-operation from batmen, etc.; he was also responsible for the condition of the gardens. But in fact there was really no need for a Mess Committee at Tangmere. The key men had been there since long before the war, and they were civilians. Bill Barrell, a retired RAF officer, had donned his Squadron Leader's uniform for the war but he was back in plain clothes performing the same duties. All that was needed was a PMC to check frivolous complaints, to ensure that officers were not rude to the servants, and to monitor the general behaviour of members. There were rules, though not an oppressive number, which most officers were unaware of. For example, it was not the done thing for a member to take a nap in his armchair after a meal – what was his bedroom for? Some messes banned the sale of strong drink in the bar before lunch, but we didn't. No matter, if officers, especially pilots, tended to drink too much at midday, this information would soon filter through to me from the head barman and other agencies, and I could either ban offenders from using the bar or invite the Station Commander to consider having them kicked out.

The Mess at Tangmere was more like a country house than a military establishment. A first class architect had been employed to construct it circa 1926. It had a low centre with an imposing hall, wide corridors leading to the ante-room, the dining hall, the billiard room, a small ladies' room, a range of lavatories, a cloakroom, and Bill Barrell's office. The public rooms were spacious with large casement windows. The kitchens extended away at the rear, but they were conveniently placed for the dining-room which was not pervaded with kitchen smells. On either side were wings containing officers' bedrooms, with plenty of bathrooms. The wing that was bombed had been long repaired, but it looked somewhat stark, so I told Job the head gardener to stick in some fast-growing Virginia creeper to match the rest of the elevation.

'I should have thought of that myself,' he grunted.

'Ah well, no one's infallible, Job.'

'Oi bloody well am, except now and again.'

There was a sweeping driveway around a circular lawn with a large round rose-bed in the middle, and a border of flowers the length of the building. A limited number of cars could be parked by the Mess, but there was a large car-park behind the building. The Mess was designed to accommodate officers from single-seater fighters, so it was not a particularly large building compared with Bomber and Coastal Command messes. The nearby coastal station of Thorney Island, for example, was the size of Blenheim Palace, and in the modern idiom just as ugly. Some half-wit had sited it so that it was necessary to cross the main runway to get to it from the entrance to the station, and this demanded traffic lights and a lot of prudence. Tucked away behind some trees to the side of Tangmere's mess was a hard tennis court, and five minutes walk away was a squash court. Inside the mess was a card room; it was not the thing to play cards in the ante-room, and in theory the only games allowed were bridge and whist. More than that, if playing for money, winnings and losses were entered in a bridge book to ensure that members were not gambling too heavily. That was really too pre-war to make sense, so I did away with the bridge book, and allowed them to play poker if they wanted. In my position as PMC I was given two large rooms, one with my bed in it, and the other as a study, or a sitting room if I wanted to invite someone up for a drink. I also had the services of the head batman, Tom Griffiths, and he could have lived very well acting as valet to a Duke with any money to spare. The only thing missing was a library although there were book cupboards available, so I appointed an officer as librarian and we started off with second-hand books.

Bill Barrell kept the accounts, monitored the head chef's budget and so forth. Members paid a mess subscription and a mess contribution. The subscription covered the cost of food over and above the official ration allowance, and if members wanted a greater variety in their diet, then the cost would be calculated and put to the vote at meetings of members. Reserve funds were also accumulated to pay for items such as more paintings on the walls. The contribution paid for daily newspapers and magazines, maintenance of the billiard table, books for the library and the rest. There was an RAF tradition, drawn from the old RFC, that after dining in nights officers should let off steam. One game was to line up a dozen officers, each with his head crouched between the thighs of the man ahead and the man in front would place his head in the belly of an officer with his back to the wall. The leader of the opposing team would take a running jump as far up the line of crouching bodies as he could, immediately followed in turn by the rest of his team. The idea was to cause the line of men to collapse under the combined weight, through the endeavours of the men on top to break them up. The teams would then change places, and the side which collapsed more often was the loser.

Then there was piggy-back fighting, where a big man would settle a lighter man on his shoulders and joust with another pair until one jockey brought the other down with a crunch. The furniture would be pushed to the side of the ante-room for these purposes to expose a fair size battlefield. Games of soccer were indulged in using cabbages as a ball, and in short time the parquet floor would become slippery as an ice rink with bits of cabbage, and many a tumble would occur. Senior officers would stand on grand pianos waving beer mugs and leading the chorus in bawdy, blasphemous, pornographic songs – my repertoire of such songs would make a eunuch blush. Inwardly I strongly disapproved of such puerile activities, but I kept my feeling to myself. At some messes I visited, fireworks were lit and thrown in indiscriminate directions, which was really asking for trouble – I certainly did not allow that sort of nonsense at Tangmere.

Before the war, dining in nights took place once a week and they were compulsory; they were analogous to parades. The idea was to allow junior officers to talk informally to seniors, also to bring in officers who lived in married quarters or off the camp. Mess kit was worn, which consisted of a stiff shirt and black bow tie, a waistcoat with RAF buttons, a monkey jacket with brass buttons, and the trousers which were termed slacks, possibly because they were extremely tight. At the bottom of the legs were straps which were fastened below the boots under the soles in order to keep the slacks tight to the legs. The boots were calf length, made of patent leather, and they had straps inside to allow them to be pulled onto the feet and legs with a gadget similar to that used for pulling on riding boots. The slacks were drawn over them to shape the lower leg, and then the slacks were strapped under them. Those who had any wore miniature medals, and all in all the dress was most uncomfortable. Wilfred and I were the only officers at Tangmere to possess mess kit, and the others wore their best uniforms with white shirts and black bow ties.

As the RAF was cut down to size, mess kit was gradually re-introduced and a uniform allowance was paid to those who bought them. My pre-war allowance for the kit was £75, but it cost me more than that. The boots alone were priced at £25, and the Lord knows what articles of such excellent workmanship would cost today. They would certainly run into hundreds of pounds. But like so many things, dining in nights had lapsed during the war, and Wilfred and I decided to reintroduce the custom, much to the delight of the permanent Mess Staff. Percy busied himself in producing a first rate menu, and under my supervision Paddy brought No 1 squadron's silver from the vaults, where it had languished during the war. It had been customary for officers leaving the squadron to present it with a silver piece, and sometimes a few officers all destined to leave at about the same time would club together and donate a rather special item. Considering that No 1 had been formed in 1908 as a balloon unit in the Army, there was a great number of trophies which I calculated to be worth £10,000 in 1946 values! I hastily detailed a squadron officer to be in charge of squadron silver, and called on Dusty Miller to find a couple of trustworthy airmen. He arrived with two men who had been apprentice silversmiths before the war.

We checked the articles against the inventory and found nothing missing. Paddy produced some silver-cleaning material and they went to work polishing the stuff. It took them three days – the rigging wires on models of biplanes are tricky indeed to clean. The officers were briefed on procedure before the first dining in night. I turned up in the ante-room at 7.30 P.M., and Mess members streamed in after me. Each officer clicked his heels to me, and selected his drink from a wine waiter with a silver salver. Beer was not offered, and sherry was *de rigueur*. The Station Commander turned up in due time and clicked his heels for this was my Mess not his, although he had Prime Ministerial authority to sack me if I didn't make a proper job of it. At the stroke of 8 P.M., Paddy, resplendent in a dinner jacket, threw open the doors and told me in a loud voice that dinner was served. We finished our drinks and I escorted Wilfred to the head table, followed by other officers not necessarily in order of seniority. A table plan showing where officers should sit was only needed on guest nights; usually they could sit with their buddies. The head table faced the windows looking onto the front of the Mess, and behind was a raised stage capable of seating a band. Wilfred was on my right and I occupied the central seat; the other more senior officers, together with Padre Hurn, occupied the rest of the head table. Two ranges of tables facing each other ran down towards the windows, and on guest nights a third could be placed between them making it possible to seat perhaps a hundred people.

Gleaming white tablecloths covered the polished wood surfaces, and strategically placed silver ornaments, including two large candelabra, added to the show. Most of the silver belonged to the squadron, but some pieces had been presented to or purchased by the Mess.

We all stood behind our chairs until everyone was assembled, I bashed my gavel on its plinth and Padre Hurn said grace. Then I sat Wilfred down and followed suit with the others. A babble of conversation began and continued until all the courses had been served. Wine waiters glided to and fro offering white or red wines, or both. Discreet note was taken of what individual officers drank, both before dinner in the ante-room and at the table. We calculated on making something of a profit on wines and other drinks, and I insisted that the wine should be of decent quality. This gave me the opportunity to attend tasting sessions at our wine merchants, and I always got the stuff at wholesale prices. When the food was consumed the tables were cleared of everything except the silver, crumbs were swept into dust pans, then Paddy produced two decanters of port ahead of me. I leant over to pour Wilfred a glass on my right, filled my own, and passed a decanter to my left for people to pour their own. Paddy speeded things up by placing another decanter ahead of the Vice President at the bottom of the table, and he passed the port strictly in a clockwise direction. Eventually a decanter would arrive back at my place and I put it in a wine coaster. Then I bashed my gavel for silence, rose and boomed, 'Mr Vice. The King.' He would get up and stutter, 'Gentlemen. The King' and we would drink the loyal toast. I had been Mr Vice on a number of occasions and it caused me no hardship. The most junior officer on the Station was selected as Mr Vice, and all he had to do was to propose the loyal toast. Yet some of these little buggers used to work themselves into a frenzy when they knew they would be Mr Vice for a night. They would suffer sleepless nights and sweat over dinner waiting for the awesome moment when they were called. When that was finished, Paddy would place a silver cigarette box and a cigar box in front of me and distribute others around the tables. I would take my time before I opened the boxes, knowing that lots of them were dying for a fag – a form of sadism I guess. Silver ashtrays were placed round the table, the port would be passed again, and coffee would be served. There would be no speeches unless an officer or officers were due to be posted from Tangmere, in which case Wilfred would thank them for their services no matter whether or not he thought their services stank. They would be expected to reply. But they were given free food and wine. On guest nights, of course, I would have to welcome the guests and all that.

The Army and Navy follow much the same rigmarole, but, as usual, the Navy have to be different. They had George III aboard a ship and when it was time for the loyal toast he was too drunk to get up, so they toasted him sitting down. They invented the yarn that the ceilings on the old sailing ships were too low to stand for the loyal toast and to this day remain seated for the toast.

CHAPTER 21

We decided to throw a guest night when we were sure that members were sufficiently well drilled in mess etiquette, and I went through the list of honorary members of the Mess. It is customary for officers messes to invite people like the local gentry and senior retired RAF officers to become honorary members. With the help of Bill Barrell, I discovered that most of our honorary members had been dead for twenty years, so I decided to make out a new list. To my horror the Duke of Richmond had never been invited, even though, through his agent, he had given Mess members honorary membership of his Goodwood Golf Club; furthermore, he had served in the RAF during the war. I immediately sent him a letter inviting him to become an honorary member when he could enjoy what facilities we had at Tangmere. Two yachting clubs, one at Itchenor, the other at Littlehampton, had offered us reduced fees for the hire of their boats, so I wrote to the Presidents and the Secretaries. Just for a lark I invited Colonel Ebenezer Pike, knowing that he didn't want the facilities of the Mess, but at least I made the gesture. That about ended my time as PMC for my wife moved down and I took a married quarter. But I think that Wilfred and I sparked a bit of the pre-war customs into wartime officers, some of whom would be selected as regulars in due course.

Then I was told that the squadron was to convert onto jet fighters in the form of Meteors Mk 3. My heart sank for I had seen the Meteor and disliked its lines intensely. In my experience, having flown more than a hundred different types of aircraft, if an aeroplane looks good to a skilled eye, it usually is good. But the Meteor looked like nothing on earth. It had twin engines, each widely spaced from the cockpit, indicating that it would be hell to handle if cither engine flamed out. The wing roots were thick so that the main spars were big enough to accept the weight of the engines. Twin engined fighters were rare. True, the Luftwaffe introduced the Messerschmitt 262 towards the end of the war, and it bore a certain resemblance to the Meteor. It caught the long-range USAAF with its trousers down simply because it was much faster than conventional fighters; but I didn't believe the Meteor had much speed advantage over the Spitfire Mk XXI, and it certainly lacked its manoeuvrability.

In my estimation a Spitfire Mk XXI in the hands of a capable pilot could have shot down five Meteors for the loss of one Spitfire. However, only a limited number of the Mk XXI was produced and it would not have been cost effective to retain the breed. Ironically, today there is a school of thought inclined to the view that souped up Spitfires should be reintroduced for battlefield purposes. Some of the advantages are ease of maintenance, the ability to take off from autobahns and land back again, using improvised servicing facilities, outstanding manoeuvrability, and comparatively high speed at low level. Modern jet fighters are stressed essentially for top speed at high level in rarefied air; they would break up if full power was used at low level. Above all, modern ground-to-air defence systems rely on heat-seeking missiles, and jet engines produce an awful lot of heat, but they would be unable to home onto the heat produced from exhaust stubs. The Air Staff have always been notoriously short-sighted in their planning, but I suppose it is difficult to point the finger of blame at them for not foreseeing such possibilities in 1946/47.

The first Meteor Mk 3 was ferried into Tangmere, and before the pilot removed one of my precious Spitfires, I asked him how to fly the bloody thing. He said he didn't know, save for the rudiments, he was just a sodding ferry pilot. He did show me how to start the engines, and pointed out that if the jet efflux temperature gauges went off the clock, that meant that the engines had caught fire. I had sent teams of skilled fitters to the factory on courses to learn how to service the engine and airframes and they were instructing the mechanics what to do. When a jet engine is started, a turbine begins to rotate which sucks air into the intakes. Kerosene fuels jets and they stink of paraffin oil. By pressing the starter button, having first opened the fuel cocks, a large sparking plug glows white-hot and the turbines, powered either by electricity from starter batteries, or later by explosive cartridges, turn. Fuel jets spurt kerosene over the spark plug and this is ignited; and hot air is sucked in by the turbine, accelerated, expanded and spouted from the efflux. By opening the throttle more kerosene is pumped into the furnace, increasing the rotation of the turbine which draws more and more air into the engine and hurls it out. There are many variations on the theme but that should suffice. A jet cannot function in space for there is insufficient oxygen for the burning process, but a rocket engine can because it carries its own liquid oxygen.

I climbed into the Meteor to find for myself how to fly it, and was immediately impressed by the forward vision, being perched high above a tricycle undercarriage – no big engine cowling to obscure my forward vision. The smell of kerosene abated when I clipped on my oxygen mask. I started the engines and gingerly opened the throttles; if I had given full throttle the burnt air would have blown down the dispersal huts. I moved onto the taxi track and found that I could steer either by using the brakes or by giving more power to one of the engines. The engines responded sluggishly to the throttles, but I worked out the solution to that when I was lined up on the runway. I applied full brakes, gently gave both engines full power and then released the brakes, whereupon she began to trundle up the runway like a lame cart-horse, but gathered speed as more and more air was sucked in by her forward movement. She took longer than a Spitfire to gather take off speed. I eased back on the stick and lifted her off the ground. I had applied fifteen degrees of flap for take off, and I retracted the undercart and the flaps after getting airborne. I eased back the throttles from full take off power, waited until we had arrived at an air speed of 270 knots and put her into a climb, maintaining that speed.

(Not long after the war the RAF rejected miles per hour as a measure of speed and used knots instead.)

What was most welcome was the absence of noise in the sealed, pressurized cockpit and the lack of vibration; the Merlin engine in the Spitfire had to turn an enormous airscrew, but although the jet turbines were rotating at 14,500 revs per minute, the Meteor ran like a sewing machine. I climbed to 35,000 feet, straightened her up and gave her full throttle. Jets give their best performance at height, for although the air is thin it is also very cold, which proportionally increases the mass of air turning the turbines. Furthermore, much less fuel is used at height – flying flat out at ground level would exhaust the fuel supply in about half an hour, but at height the endurance would be approximately one and a half hours. Tactically this was unsound and presupposed that intruding enemy aircraft would fly at great height, which was not necessarily so. It didn't matter a damn in a Spitfire whether one made an interception high or low from a fuel consumption aspect, apart from the use of petrol on the climb.

I put her into a dive and she quickly gained speed since she had no propeller to create drag. Then I hauled her up into a loop to which she easily responded, having plenty of speed for the purpose. The aileron control was sluggish compared with the quick reactions of the Spitfire, which presented another tactical defect. Then I reduced speed, throttled one engine back to idling revs and opened the other throttle wide. Without the slightest warning she flicked onto her back and tried to fall in an incipient spin. I hastily throttled back the other engine, rolled her out and dived to gain speed before opening both throttles. Although my reaction was immediate, I noted that I lost 3,000 feet in height during all this. I don't like spinning aeroplanes for they are out of control, and the pilot has to work hard to correct them. It was fun in the old biplanes, but not in monoplanes. Sometimes aircraft refuse to come out of a spin for no apparent reason, and it is often impossible to bale out as the pilot is hurled from one side of the cockpit to the other. The introduction of rocket ejection seats helps in such conditions, but when I went up in one my back was permanently injured. Jet engines occasionally flame out, possibly because of dirt affecting the fuel filters, and there is a relighting drill. The fuel cock must be closed down, speed reduced, an emergency button pressed which causes a stand-by sparking plug to glow, the throttle opened slightly, then the fuel cock is opened. But the system was by no means infallible. I have been President of three Boards of Enquiry enquiring into how Meteor pilots were killed. They were all caused by failure of the relighting system, combined with the pilots' inability to control a Meteor on one engine. Yet the Canberra bomber, a blown-up version of the Meteor, is perfectly safe on one engine unless the pilot is suffering from delirium tremens.

As I thought about descending to land I noticed a lever by the throttle quadrant which nobody had told me about. It wasn't marked red for danger so I pulled it to see what happened, where-upon the aircraft shuddered like a maiden aunt about to be raped. It didn't seem to be a bale out situation and I looked out of the canopy and saw an aerofoil with holes in it at an angle of ninety degrees extended from the wing surface. There was another one on the other wing and when I pushed the lever they both retracted leaving clean wing surfaces. I then saw that the Meteor had lost a lot of speed in short time, clearly due to these aerofoils. I racked my brain and it was clear that they were intended to decelerate the aircraft, and they had spoiled the airflow over the wing surfaces thus creating drag. I soon found out the reason for their existence when I turned her on her back, hauled back the stick to put her into a vertical dive. I throttled back and eased her out of the dive, but she continued to dive without much reduction of speed. It then occurred to me that there was nothing to check her since she had no propeller to create drag. I extended the airflow spoilers, or dive brakes as they are termed, and she quickly lost speed to the extent that I had to give her engine power to maintain my angle of descent.

I arrived at 1,500 feet three miles east of the runway, retracted the dive brakes and gave her full throttle aiming at the squadron dispersal huts. We passed over them at fifty feet making a lot of noise. I hauled her up in a vertical climb, performed four upward charlies and stall-turned as she ran out of flying speed. Then I sidled back and joined the circuit. The short runway was in use even though the wind was light, and I had to approach over the Goodwood Downs which didn't give me much room to lose height to ground level. I touched down just beyond the runway threshold on the main wheels and let the nose-wheel drop. She roared along the runway showing little inclination to slow down, but I didn't want to use the brakes until she had slowed down for in all probability they would have begun to burn from excess friction. I put out the dive brakes but they didn't help because they were only effective when flying reasonably fast. As we devoured more and more of the runway, something dramatic had to be done about it, so I gave her short blasts of brake, sponging them on and off in an attempt to ensure that they didn't get red-hot. I began to run out of runway and in desperation applied full brakes, which brought her to a halt just ahead of ploughland. I turned off the runway steering by applying power to one engine, and stayed put for a quarter of an hour with the brakes off. They were white hot, and if anyone had thrown a bucket of water over them they would have exploded. Then, steering by engines I taxied back to the dispersal. The pilots ganged up and asked me what they were like to fly. I said it was a piece of cake.

CHAPTER 22

The trick when landing Meteors and some other jets is to touch down on the main wheels and keep the nose wheel high in the air until the aircraft slows down to the extent that forces of gravity cause the nose wheel to drop onto the runway of its own accord. In that attitude the drag of the wings themselves acts as an effective braking system. It wasn't long before all the pilots were converted to Meteors and we were flying our daily routine, practising tactics, flight and squadron formation flying, armament training and the rest. To fly accurately in formation required more anticipation than in Spitfires, for the jets were comparatively sluggish in responding to slight altera-tions in power settings necessary for the art. I found it useful to flick the dive brakes in and out when in formation with other pilots – it is always a good thing for flying leaders to keep their hand in at formation flying.

I thought about establishing a formation aerobatic team, but on reflection decided not to. The Meteor Mk 3 didn't have enough reserves of power for such intricacies. But as the aircraft gave its best performance at height, the order of the day was to fly towards the tropopause (the imaginary boundary between the lower stratum of the atmosphere and the stratosphere) and carry out practice interceptions high above the ground. Similarly, long range cross-country navigation flights could only be at high level, else they would have been short range navigation flights, but we did use our allocated low flying areas for map-reading exercises at half throttle. The trouble was that if we tried to fly to the extremity of our radii of action at high level, more often than not it was necessary to climb through cloud. Pilots could ascertain whether or not they had arrived over their pin-points by checking their position with the radar operators. To get the best from these exercises, the practice was to land with only five minutes fuel left in the tanks. But the homing and landing aids had improved very little since the end of the war, and I laid it down that pilots should have enough fuel left to make diversionary landings at nearby airfields if Tangmere's weather suddenly clamped down. I also had to rule that Meteors were not to fly if the cloud base was less than 700 feet, whereas we flew our Spitfires with a cloud base of 500 feet, or less on occasions. Another order was that pilots were not to flame out an engine; they could practise single engine flying with one engine throttled right back. But relighting drill was assiduously practised and checked by the flight commanders on the ground. By taking such precautions, No 1 squadron never had a flying accident while I was in command.

The spring of 1947 brought with it a side-splitting belly laugh, when the Air Ministry decided that the RAF should establish a world speed record at low level. What they overlooked was that Britain was five years behind America in high speed aircraft design; and when the French aircraft industry was re-established after the war, they soon surpassed us as well. By stealing secrets the Russians were able to do the same. When the motor car first appeared on the roads in Britain, it was deemed necessary that a man with a red flag should walk ahead of the vehicle, which therefore moved at walking pace. Before that, when the railways were constructed, learned gentlemen made solemn pronouncements to the effect that the human body would disintegrate if it were moved along at over 50 mph. The British have deep-seated objections to change, so naturally enough when it was clear that aircraft could be designed to exceed the speed of sound – Mach 1 – the scientists and aeromedicos in the Air Ministry were adamant that pilots would indeed disintegrate in the process. Aircraft design on supersonic aircraft was held back. Instead, their efforts were concentrated on supersonic rockets fitted with measuring equipment which were launched from aircraft near places like the Scilly Isles. The Meteor was subsonic, as was it's successor, the Hunter, which entered squadron service in the early 1950s. The hideous night fighter Javelin, which could only have been designed by Heath Robinson, was also subsonic, and so were the V bombers. Of course the Americans were flying supersonic while Britain was playing tiddly-winks, and in the Korean War, circa 1950, American and Soviet-built fighters were indulging in the first supersonic dogfights in world history. In about 1958, the American Hustler bomber flew non-stop, using in-flight refuelling, to Japan at a mean speed of 1,500 mph – twice the speed of sound!

I had a fair knowledge of all this, and I wept with laughter when I learned that the High Speed Flight was to attempt to exceed 600 mph over a measured course. Their aircraft were Meteors Mk 4 with more powerful engines than the Mk 3, and they had not yet entered squadron service. The pilots were Group Captain Teddy Donaldson, Bill Warburton, chief test pilot of the Gloster Aircraft Company, and Squadron Leader Neville Duke who was just about the best test pilot going. The ground crews wore flashy white overalls, and the gentlemen of the Press abounded to find out who would be 'the fastest man on earth'. Well, I reckon I reached about 600 mph when I put a Spitfire into a vertical dive at full boost when being chased by a gaggle of Messerschmitts. Certainly the stressed skin on the wings was buckled when I landed, and the Spitfire was a write-off because the main spars were out of alignment. If this was supposed to be a public relations operation showing the world the tremendous efficiency of Britain's air defences then that was inverted logic. What it displayed, in fact, was that Britain had a force of clapped-out obsolescent fighters in the front line.

The course was laid on close to the shore off Bognor, and international observers took up position with measuring equipment in strategic positions. The Meteors were polished before every flight, in the hope that this would cut down air friction and add another knot or two to the speed. Teddy Donaldson did the first few runs without success, and failed to gain sufficient air speed. Bill Warburton had a shot without success. Neville Duke, who could fly the pants off both of them, had been kept in the background, but when he was allowed a shot he neatly broke the record. But unfortunately, probably because he had not been given enough practice runs, he dived slightly as he went into his final leg. This was against the rules and he was disqualified. All in all it was a pathetic, expensive, time-consuming charade. Teddy eventually kept to the rules and won the record.

Towards the end of 1947 my time with No 1 squadron was running out. This coincided with a government economy measure which effectively halved the front line strength of Fighter Command. The folly of this was demonstrated a year later when the Russians blockaded Berlin, thereby bringing the Soviets and the West into an eyeball-to-eyeball confrontation. But the Air Staff was never very good at strategic planning. They were never very good at anything that I can think of. The changed policy meant that fighter squadrons would be reduced to a cadre basis, meaning that half the squadron would be disbanded. This meant that I was no longer in command of a squadron, merely a flight. So I was not altogether displeased when I was selected to go to Holland as Air Defence Adviser to the Dutch Government.

My only nagging thought was that it was unlikely that I would ever see much of Tangmere again. By now it was my spiritual home.

CHAPTER 23

The Dutch Air Ministry was contained in a requisitioned hotel at Scheveningen, the seaside town a couple of miles from The Hague. I shared an office with the Chief of Staff, Col. van Geissen, which adjoined that of the Chief of the Air Staff, General Aler. I had been given a posh flat in The Hague large enough for my wife and myself, our children and a nanny. The Dutch liked Britons because they and the Canadians had liberated Holland, which is why they preferred British military advisers and were prepared to buy British military hardware. They were mighty short of dollars in any case, and Britain was prepared to lend them sterling at reasonable rates. The fascination of my job was how to start an air force from virtually nothing. Although Anton Fokker was a Dutchman he designed his First War aeroplanes for the Germans. The story goes that he first offered the designs of the unique *Eindecker* to the British General Staff who were in charge of the RFC, but as they didn't know the difference between an aeroplane and a kite they turned him away. In World War I Holland was neutral and had no air force to speak of. In World War II the Luftwaffe shot down the small obsolete Dutch Air Force in twenty-four hours. In the Dutch East Indies Dutch pilots were attached to British and American squadrons with a role confined to sea reconnaissance. Some Dutch pilots escaped to Britain and flew with RAF squadrons, but all in all there was precious little experience to draw on.

Holland had had a rough time in the war and little money was available for defence. General Aler was a shrewd hombre, and indeed when he left the Air Force he was appointed President of KLM. When I left the RAF I flew with every international airline company in the world, save for the Soviet bloc, and I used to work out a system of marks indicating the excellence or lack of it of the airlines. Marks were awarded for punctuality, the quality of the food, and even the trim of the stewardesses. KLM came out top. Sad to say BOAC ranked only sixth. But the first piece of advice I gave the General was to form a lobby to squeeze more money from the government for the Air Force. Traditionally the Navy took pride of place in Holland, and I wrote a paper providing him with ammunition showing that warships were vulnerable without sufficient air support, so priorities needed radical revision.

I visited all the airfields where I found mainly training aircraft plus a few Spitfires and miscellaneous types. Conditions were generally poor and consequently morale was low. Most of the airmen were conscripts called up for a year, and I pointed out that this was fairly stupid, also a waste of money, because it took a year to become productive, whereupon they left. This was highly political, and I left Aler to find his way through that maze. I was paid as usual by the Air Ministry, who claimed the money back from the Dutch Ministry of Finance under contract. I discovered that I was paid more than Aler himself and told him that was bloody ludicrous, that something had to be done with the pay structure as a whole. He told me that there was a shortage of money all round, and what funds there were had been granted for massive projects such as reclaiming the Zuider Zee from the sea. I couldn't have a new, modern Dutch Air Force tomorrow, but there was no harm in making the attempt.

The first thing to do was to plan for a radar chain, and it would be economical to use underground German control rooms as operations centres. The technicalities of siting radar stations were beyond me, so I arranged for a team of RAF specialists to come over and draw up plans. Aler detailed some of his Signals Staff to discuss matters with the British, and I said I would also sit in in case they tried to pull a fast one. Was I British or Dutch he enquired? Professionally, I replied, he could consider me to be Dutch. And he did too!

In due course the question arose, what sort of jet aircraft should they buy from Britain? NATO had not then been formed, but it seemed to me that America would have to enter the ring sooner or later, and then the Dutch Air Force would be equipped with US aircraft. I looked on the existing British types as short term investments, useful for training pilots and ground crew in jet techniques and little more. The only alternatives were the Meteor Mk 4 and the Vampire, and I suggested to Aler that I should go to the factories and evaluate each type. The Meteor Mk 4 was just a souped-up version of the Mk 3 which I knew all about, but the Vampire was quite different. It was a little single seat fighter with one engine, nice to fly but underpowered. I reported back to Aler and told him to contract for the Vampire. I explained that its speed and climb ability were below that of the Meteor, but that wasn't really important; it was certainly good enough for use as a jet conversion vehicle, and it was more manoeuvrable than the Meteor. Being single engined it was easier to fly than the other, and pilots would need less time to convert in the class rooms. It was much simpler to maintain and squadrons would require fewer engine and airframe mechanics. Finally, each aircraft would cost a sight less than a Meteor. Aler cross-examined me at length. Another factor I brought in was that the Vampire could operate from shorter airfields than the Meteor, which again would save costs. Why, with a bit of luck he could force through a budget to get his jets without much trouble. I then reclined in the armchair and waited for his reaction, which was to walk to a cabinet and take out a bottle of Dutch gin and two glasses. Dutch gin, Bols Geneva and the like, is pretty powerful stuff and tastes like castor oil. One can add spice to it by mixing in a little *créme de menthe,* but I can hold my own drinking it raw – I had to learn pretty fast.

He handed me a full glass, poured one for himself, sat down and put his feet on the desk. We demolished the bottle before I left.

'You don't know much about Dutch politics,' he said. 'You don't know that I've been pacing the corridors of power taking your name in vain, telling those buggers in government that my British expert who is advised by your Air Ministry, has been giving me urgent advice to do this that and the other.'

'I'm not working from an Air Ministry brief!' I protested. 'I just tell you what I think.'

'I know,' he replied, 'which is why I trust you. I wouldn't trust your bloody Air Ministry though. Anyway, although I agree with everything you said, I'm going for a contract to equip my Air Force with Meteors.'

'That's entirely up to you, Sir. But you'll have difficulty in getting the money.'

'Money is the whole point. I've obtained agreement in principle to re-equip with jets. The fact that overheads for Meteors are greater than those of Vampires means that they will have to give me more money. Having been granted a higher than necessary budget will mean that it will be easier to raise it in due course. Of course, I will say that my RAF adviser strongly recommended Meteors. They've never heard of Vampires, so don't mention them to anybody. Have another drink and tell me what's wrong with my Air Force.'

'"In matters of commerce the fault of the Dutch / Is offering too little and asking too much,"' I quoted.

'Yes. Your Prime Minister, Canning, said that. But he also went on to say: "The French are with equal advantage content, / So we clap on Dutch bottoms just twenty per cent." Which is why I don't trust your bloody Air Ministry.'

He was a clever devil was General Aler.

My original contract to work for the Dutch was for two years, but when that was up they asked me to stay for another six months, and when that was up they asked me to stay for a further six months. What I had been with them for three years they asked me to stay for another six months, but by that time I was getting itchy feet and declined. The whole of the Staff joined in and gave me a farewell booze-up, and they all signed two big albums filled with photographs of Dutch scenes. I knew all the places and buildings for we had thoroughly explored Holland from the Frans Hals gallery in Haarlem where he lived and worked, to the new Van Gogh gallery near Arnhem. Queen Juliana made me a Commander of the ancient Order of the Orange Nassau with the Swords. It was an enjoyable interlude.

CHAPTER 24

I went to see the Personnel people at the Air Ministry and they asked me what sort of job I would prefer. I said I would like a flying job and they told me not to be so bloody silly – I had already had more than enough flying jobs. An altercation blew up, and they confessed that they had two flying vacancies, one as Officer in charge of flying at Church Fenton in Yorkshire which didn't appeal to me in the least, the other as OC Flying at Tangmere which was highly satisfactory save for one thing. OC Flying was a new appointment where the incumbent would look after the airfield as a whole, including ATC procedures, and generally keep the squadron commanders on the right rails. As a squadron commander, if anyone told me how to keep on the right rails I would have told him to go jump in the river wearing a cement jacket, and I didn't fancy interfering with other squadron commanders unless they made a pig's breakfast of things. However, I told them to start the paperwork rolling to get me to Tangmere, and then went to see the boss man who was an old chum of mine. He said I was very lucky to be given another flying job, and I pointed out that I had just spent three years flying a desk in Holland and I needed to get back to flying aeroplanes.

Then I asked him which squadrons were at Tangmere, and he told me No 1 was still there, and No 43 squadron had recently been re-established. I asked him who commanded No 43 and I knew the chap well. I pointed out to my chum that the present incumbent was quite a bit senior to me, and it would be a hollow laugh if I tried to boss him around. In any case, he was an awkward cuss. In all logic, he should be put in charge of flying and I should take over No 43.

'If I let you command 43 squadron,' he said with a chuckle, 'that would mean you'll have commanded more squadrons than anyone else in RAF history!'

'*In omnibus princeps*,' I replied.

'What the hell does that mean?'

'It means there's got to be a first time for everything.'

'Why couldn't you say it in English?'

'Because it's No 1 squadron's motto.'

'Well, supposing we kick Tony Brown upstairs as OC Flying and he tried to tell you how to run 43 squadron?'

'He's only senior to me on paper; we hold the same rank. I'd shoot him.'

'All right, we'll play it that way.'

'Jolly good. I'll take you out for a drink. I'll pay.'

I had a heady drive down to Tangmere where I clocked in at the Mess. Bill Barrell knew I was coming and had given me a decent room, and also wangled things and made Tom Griffiths my batman. He unpacked my suitcases and I visited senior members of the Mess Staff, who were as pleased to see me as I was to see them. I drove to Chichester, had a chat and a meal with Arthur King at the Unicorn and returned to the Mess for an early night. I wasn't part of the Station until I reported to the Station Commander, which I did at 0900 hours sharp the next day. He looked me up and down and I did likewise to him. I liked what I saw.

Tom Prickett was a tall, large man with a rubicund face, dark hair, deep-set, very shrewd eyes, an easy grin and a habit of putting his hand over his mouth when he giggled, rather like a naughty schoolboy. He had an easygoing manner, but I didn't fancy the notion of getting on the wrong side of him. He introduced himself and sat me down.

'I gather you're a bit of a legend round here,' he said. 'The Mess Staff went on a boozer when they heard you were coming.'

'I know Tangmere very well,' I informed him. 'I was PMC for a time in 1946.'

'Yes, and you also commanded No 1 squadron. How come you're back here three years after leaving it to take on No 43?'

'The mills of God grind slowly,' I pointed out. 'But they grind exceedingly small.'

'I think you've been fiddling the system,' he accused. 'Tony Brown is hopping mad at having to give up command of No 43. He only took command a few months ago when it was reformed.'

'I don't know how to fiddle the system, Sir,' I bleated. 'I'm too dim for that. Anyway, I don't see what Tony Brown is mad about. He's senior to me and he's been given a more important appointment than that of squadron commander.'

'Do you really believe that OC Flying is more important than commanding a squadron – especially one with No 43's background?'

'No I don't. I think it's a load of bullshit. I did the job and looked after No 1 squadron at the same time.'

'That's what he thinks. I foresee a bit of friction between you two.'

'Don't worry about that, Sir. I've got a wistful charm. Even sharks allow me to pull their teeth out.'

'Don't be so bloody impertinent. Come on, I'll take you to the squadron and introduce you to your flight commanders.'

We arrived at the dispersal; 1 squadron still occupied the huts it had when I was with it, but this one was better placed. I met the flight commanders, Steve Daniel and Freddie Lister, both of whom had medals for gallantry;

they were a hardened pair of experienced toughies who viewed me with grave suspicion. Suddenly someone bawled: 'HE'S GOING IN!' I turned towards the dispersal hut to see who was going in. When I turned my head the Station Commander and the flight commanders were driving hell bent along the perimeter track. I hi-jacked a car and followed them to the playing fields where I saw a Meteor jammed between the rugby posts on its belly. The pilot was standing by looking somewhat dazed, and I noticed the aircraft bore the markings of No 43 squadron, which were black and white chequers painted on the fuselage. It was clear from the skid marks that it had all but removed the roof of the Station Commander's residence. I saw enough, left the others to sort out the mess and drove back to the dispersal. I walked through the pilots' room to my office, noting that the whole place needed the same treatment I had given to No 1 squadron's dispersal. I began to throw out the muck in the desk drawers when the telephone rang.

'This is the Senior Air Staff Officer, 11 Group. Is that the Officer Commanding 43 squadron.'

'Hardly,' I replied. 'I've only been here for ten minutes.'

'Congratulations,' the voice announced.

'On what?'

'For being the first chap to let one of his aircraft prang ten minutes after he assumed command.'

This could be only one voice, and it belonged to Rupert Leigh, my first squadron commander in 1940. I had seen him on and off since he left 66 squadron, but not often.

'Rupert, you old bastard,' I exclaimed. 'How are you?'

'You can't call me a bastard; I'm an Air Commodore now.'

'Suits you very well – a closet full of wind.'

'You mean commode, you illiterate sod. Toss you for half a crown. Heads or tails?'

136

'Tails,' I said.

'You win. I'll put one in the post. Let me have a report on that accident when you've sorted things out.'

Rupert and I tossed for money over the telephone on numerous occasions, and the loser posted the stakes. I'm not a betting man, but Rupert is an inveterate gambler; he'd bet on anything. But it was a point of honour to dib up if you lost.

I spent the day sniffing things out and was unhappy at what I found. Morale was none too high, although the flight commanders were of high calibre and so were the SNCOs I met. The dispersal huts were shabby, as were those of the servicing crews; and the barrack block was almost as bad as was No 1's when I moved the squadron to Tangmere. The Flight Sergeant Discip had no stature, and kept metaphorically washing his hands with soap. He was full of bullshit and bangmearse, but his executive authority hardly existed. I had the flight commanders in and told them there was going to be a bloody great clean-up before I concentrated on flying, and explained what form it would take. They were enthusiastic, and I asked them why the hell they hadn't got on with such things of their own volition before. Within the limits of discretion their answer was clear. My predecessor had given no encouragement, and there were indications that he was heartily disliked by the squadron as a whole. I told them we would start operation clean-up next day, and they would have to ease up on the flying until things were straightened out. They smiled and said it wouldn't be difficult to ease up on the flying; the utilization rate per aircraft was low enough as it was. Squadron personnel went back to their messes at the end of the day and I stayed behind making a few notes. There was a rap on the door which nearly broke the woodwork and Dusty Miller made a military entry. I sat him down and asked him what he wanted.

'It's good to see you again, Sir, the noo,' he said wiping his eyes.

'You too, Dusty. But what the hell do you want here. You belong to No 1 squadron.'

'They are a bloody shower, Sir,' he moaned. 'I want a compassionate posting to 43 squadron.'

'Are you drunk?'

'Not yet, Sir, but I'll die if you don't get me in with you. My present squadron commander doesn't understand me.'

'That doesn't surprise me. But don't be daft. I can't whip you away from 1 squadron just like that. What the hell would your squadron commander think? Anyway it wouldn't be fair on my present Flight Sergeant Discip.'

'That bastard's no' good enough for you. He'd let you down as soon as look at you. I've half a mind to hit him on the head with a whisky bottle.'

'I bet it would be an empty one! I'll tell you what I'll do. I'll review the position in a year's time. I simply can't try anything on at this stage.'

'I'll bloody well be dead in a year's time,' he bleated.

'In which case I'll come to your funeral and pour whisky over your grave once a week. Now shove off.'

Fate wanders up mysterious byways. He was indeed back in the fold within a year.

CHAPTER 25

I went to see Tom Prickett the next morning and told him I would write a report on the near-fatal flying accident that day for him to forward up through channels. I also said that my priority was to have a blitz on cleaning up the squadron accommodation before concentrating on flying.

He didn't say anything, but the gleam in his eyes indicated his approval. He hadn't been boss of Tangmere for long, and he was not the sort of chap to wave new brooms around at a moment's notice. He got his way by dropping polite hints, which became broader if things didn't start to move in the right direction. If in due time there was no movement, then God help the offender. Slowly, slowly catchee monkey was Tom's axiom, and it is a good one. I had to work hard to curb my impatience to follow that line. He had obviously been biding his time before putting a flea in the ear of my predecessor, and now it occurred that I was dropping the package on his lap. Somehow things usually dropped on Tom's lap, due to his stolid personality combined with his general charisma. He was a bit of a witch, not to say he stuck pins in wax figures at home, but anyone with any sense could read his mind and progress in the direction he desired. As the direction he pointed at coincided with my own, we got along splendidly.

I examined the offending pilot's log and noted with surprise, because I already knew the cause of the accident, that he was an experienced Meteor pilot; indeed he had been an instructor on the type. I called him into my office, he gave me a sloppy salute, and when I shook his hand it was limp and wet as a jellied eel. I told him to sit down. He was a big, lumbering man with seemingly slow reactions, who had to think hard before answering questions. He wasn't the right shape, and didn't seem to have the temperament to be a fighter pilot, though in the end he turned out to be reasonably average at the job. He held the rank of Flight Lieutenant, though I would never have dreamed of appointing him a flight commander. I asked him what went wrong.

He explained that he had been detailed to practise relighting drill at 20,000 feet, and he flamed out one or the other engine and relit them satisfactorily on half a dozen occasions. Then one engine refused to relight, so he burned off fuel before coming in for a single engine landing. He misjudged the approach and was in danger of stalling before he arrived over the runway threshold, so he gave the Meteor's good engine full power with the intention of throttling back when he was in safe range of the runway. Whereupon, despite his efforts to push on full opposite rudder and full aileron, the aircraft flicked over onto its back at 100 feet. He had plenty of strength in his legs and arms, but he would have needed the muscles of three gorillas to cope in that situation! He had managed to regain flying speed, and at the last possible moment he turned the Meteor over after throttling right back, managed to turn towards the playing fields, and belly-landed. He was very sorry about it.

I looked at him. He was clearly still suffering from shock, not surprisingly since he knew better than anybody he had escaped death by millimetres. He had a sizeable piece of plaster on his forehead covering a nasty gash, whereas in theory his splattered brains should have been contained in a jam jar. His name was George Strutt and he was a nice chap, so I took it gently.

'You are to be congratulated, George, on quick reactions in regaining control of your aircraft and belly-landing in such a confined space – incidentally, you scored a try on the rugby pitch. But you also all but removed most of the Station Commander's house.'

'I know, Sir, I pulled up to avoid the chimneys then she stalled on me.'

'Well, let's take it in sequence. Your failure to relight was by reason of technical causes for which you can't be blamed. I suppose relighting drill is constantly practised in the squadron.'

'Yes, Sir. Every pilot should be capable of landing on one engine.'

'Well you weren't, for starters, and you were an instructor. A bad case of pilot error. There is no need to flame out to practise single engine flying. All that is necessary is to throttle one engine right back. That will be the drill in this squadron from now on.'

'Flame outs are laid down in the training manuals,' he pointed out.

'Bugger the training manuals. I run this squadron, not the Air Ministry. Then you badly misjudged your approach, you were much too low. If you'd had sufficient height you wouldn't have had to use any power at all. You should always pretend that a single engine landing is a glide landing. Come in too high until you're sure of reaching the runway, then lose height and speed using your dive brakes and flaps *before* lowering your undercart.'

'Before lowering the undercarriage! That isn't in the training manuals.'

I glared at him and he shut up.

'Have you got any domestic problems?' I enquired.

He hesitated before he blurted it out. He had been engaged, but recently his fiancée had jilted him. It was the old, old story that I'd met so often before. I suppose most people have a nagging worry, but all a pilot must do while he's airborne is concentrate on flying his aircraft. Whether or not his bank manager is likely to foreclose on his account must simply be shoved into the unconscious part of the brain. If he killed himself his people would have a sight more to worry about than whatever may have been nagging him.

'Where does she live?' I asked.

'Norfolk,' he said.

'Right, I'll arrange for the MO to give you a fortnight's sick leave provided you go to Cornwall. I advise you to book in at the Droskyn Castle Hotel, Perranporth, but if you do make sure you've got a bundle of contraceptives.

141

You'd certainly have needed them when I last stayed there in 1942. My God! some of my bastards must now be eight years of age.'

I wrote a report explaining the circumstances of the crash, strongly recommending that flame out drill was banned. No notice was taken of this, of course, and a further fifty or so Meteors pranged before the type was phased out. I stated that I had pointed out the error of his ways to the pilot, that he had shown considerable finesse in belly-landing the aircraft, and that no disciplinary action should be taken. He had suffered enough from his fearsome experience. Tom Prickett endorsed the report and it finished up at the Air Ministry unamended.

Of course the Clerk of Works, the Barrack Warden and the head gardener knew that I was back at Tangmere: bad news travels fast, and they put up only slight resistance against my demands to convert and paint the dispersal and barrack block. We had a two seater Meteor Mk 7, useful for practising instrument flying under a hood which was pulled down in flight leaving the pilot in the front with no outside vision while the other acted as look-out. It was handy for all sorts of purposes. To add a little spice to the bait of free whisky, I offered to take all three of my old friends up for a flip. To a man they declined, stating that in twenty-five years at Tangmere they had seen so many aircraft crashes that nothing would induce them to leave terra firma. But the job was soon done, and everybody took more pride in the squadron with so much paint splashed around. There were oil drums and rusted motor cars behind the huts to be disposed of. Westhampnett was now a car racing track and a very popular one at that. The Duke of Richmond eventually closed it down when racing cars could attain speeds at which the course was unsafe; it is now a private airfield for use by club aircraft and charter flights. But I went to see the Clerk of the Course of the race track and explained that our squadron colours consisted of black and white chequers, so would he give me a couple of flags used to indicate the winner of a race. He did and we pulled one up the flag pole outside my office below my squadron commander's pennant. A large notice board was also erected announcing that No 43 (FIGHTER) SQUADRON was in residence. Our squadron badge displayed a fighting cock over the motto *Gloria Finis*, meaning it's a lovely way to die. Courage breweries also used a fighting cock as their company emblem, so I wrote to them and asked for their co-operation. They sent me models of fighting cocks until the place was littered with them. We obtained as our squadron mascot a bantam cock named Cockie, and he spent his time strutting around the gardens in front of the dispersal, occasionally flying onto the squadron notice board to relieve himself.

Cockfighting is strictly illegal in this country, but it continues especially in the mining areas of Wales and Northumberland. It so happened that there was an armament practice camp at RAF Acklington, north of Newcastle and near to Alnwick, to which squadrons were attached for a fortnight each year to exercise the cannon aimed at high speed drogues and ground targets. On the moors south of the Tyne were the ground targets, comprised of rusty old tanks and derelict Army MT. On one occasion I was making an attack when one of my cannon ran away, meaning that it wouldn't stop firing when I removed my thumb from the firing button. Here was a pretty pickle for, as I crested a hill, ahead of me lay a village. There was only one thing to do, which was to put the Meteor in a vertical climb at full throttle until the offending cannon ran out of ammunition. Certainly the shell, some of it with explosive heads, would have to fall somewhere, but by using this tactic I reckon it all dropped within the confines of the range danger area. While we were there I infiltrated a miners' club making discreet enquiries about fighting cocks. I was viewed with the gravest suspicion, but I had had a number of lapel badges of the squadron crest manufactured for the airmen to wear when in plain clothes, just to prove to the world that they belonged to a crack fighter squadron.

The miners relaxed and I was taken along secret alleys and escorted through fields to a number of large coops. An enormous fighting cock was hauled out by the scruff of its neck for my approval. I said he'd do me fine.

'Arh,' my friends said. 'Boot 'e'll need thrrree 'ens to keep 'im going. 'E be a randy sod.'

I gave them a tenner and they gave me a huge basket and dumped it in my car. We knocked up a large chicken coop which carried the birds back to Tangmere in a three ton lorry. They were let out regularly for exercise, and Cockie quickly learned to take swift evasive action.

From then on the squadron was known as The Fighting Cocks.

CHAPTER 26

I deliberately disassociated myself from No 1 squadron, although several of the SNCOs had served under me. In my view the squadron had gone downhill since my day, which Dusty Miller certainly affirmed. It seemed to lack *élan* and sparkle in keeping with the squadron commander, who took his duties seriously and rarely smiled. Furthermore, he went by the book, whereas I metaphorically threw the book out of the window. In any case it was necessary for me to stand aloof from No 1 else it might have caused some embarrassment. Nor was the squadron commander too pleased when our flying hours as indicated on the monthly returns began to shoot up, and easily exceeded his utilization rate. We also began to overfly the airfield in unusual parade formations, whereas our rivals hardly ever put up a squadron formation.

For example, I was looking through one of our pre-war photograph albums depicting squadron scenes, when one caught my eye. There was a great stack of such albums dating from World War I which were held in the Mess vaults for safe keeping. This one was of a biplane formation flown in the shape of a cross. I sketched it on a piece of paper and pondered the problem of how to position the squadron in similar formation. Times had changed, and the manner in which our predecessors had managed it would have nothing to do with jet fighters. The overriding factor of course, was to avoid the possibility of mid-air collisions.

I came to the conclusion that the formation would have to comprise thirteen aircraft. In my leading section there would be five Meteors forming into vic after take off, four in the following section, followed by three. We would climb to 15,000 feet, a safe height, before levelling off. I would maintain an easterly heading for about fifty miles and turn on a reciprocal heading towards Tangmere. Two pilots would follow in the Meteor Mk 7 to observe from above and report to me if any particular pilot was slightly out of position, whereupon I would tell him to move in or out, drop back or move forward. When I was on course for base, pilots would fall into loose formation before the gymnastics. My Nos two and three would adopt line astern formation on command, and Nos four and five were to keep well clear of the squadron until instructed otherwise. The flight commander's section behind mine was to form line abreast formation and close in on the tail of my arse end charlie. The last section was to form line astern formation and close up on the aircraft ahead. At that stage

I would instruct my Nos four and five to form up in line abreast formation to the starboard and port respectively of the middle section.

I took plenty of time to order changes in formation because this was something new and intricate for the pilots, and no squadron had attempted it in modern times. Although I had carefully briefed the pilots using a blackboard, there is a difference between theory and practice. On the first run over Tangmere there was a certain amount of jostling, and I split the formation up before we overflew the airfield. Getting back into the preliminary formation wasn't too difficult. I called my section into vic, the flight commander behind did likewise, and the other flight commander followed suit, then they closed up behind me. However, I found that I could not alter course by more than one degree without putting the cross formation into turmoil, but fortunately Cathode Ray Detection Finding equipment (CRDF) had been installed in the ATC tower. By transmitting to the tower, a signal was automatically picked up and displayed on the CRDF tube in the form of a bright light showing my exact track from the airfield. Thus the controller could tell me immediately if I was a mere half degree off track when I asked for homing assistance. By frequently transmitting, I could thus make slight alterations of course to counter wind drift.

On the second run, the spotters flying above the formation advised that only a few aircraft were out of formation, so I decided to display the cross to ground observers at Tangmere. When we had formed up I went into an easy dive and applied more power, but the pilots coped well enough. We passed over our dispersal fast and at 1,000 feet, in front of the noses of No 1 squadron. That caused them even more anguish.

I telephoned the editor of *Flight*, the aeronautical magazine, and told him that if he sent a photographer and a reporter to Tangmere we would give him a scoop. We put the photographer in the back of a Meteor Mk 7 and demonstrated our cross formation. When we landed, he explained that the cross formation was fine, but not for photographic purposes. He also said that he had taken the original cross formation photographs of the Fighting Cocks in their biplanes circa 1931, so I wasn't prepared to argue with him. I gave him the use of the blackboard to show us how he wanted to fake the formation, and instead of having the aircraft in true line abreast formation, he wanted them slightly echeloned. We took him up again and he produced some perfect, if faked, photographs. In due course *Flight* published them together with a two page spiel on the Fighting Cocks, and the old biplane cross formation pictures. As *Flight* was read in every Mess in the RAF and elsewhere, this was an excellent public relations operation which sent our rivals into a paroxysm of envy. I felt a bit guilty about it, but either they could pull their fingers out or not.

Then I decided to form a flight aerobatic team in the old tradition. The Meteor Mk 4 had enough power, and although response to the ailerons was sluggish it was worth a try. We were very careful, and began by sending experienced pilots off with rookies as their wing men, flying in pairs. The leaders went into high gee steep turns, and the wing men had to maintain close formation on them. Provided their performance was satisfactory, the leaders would take them into barrel rolls which, unlike slow rolls proper, avoid negative gee. In a slow roll aircraft are held upside down, pilots hanging in their safety harnesses, and the controls are reversed compared with straight and level flight. We weren't prepared to risk that. Some rookies were safe enough at that stage, but those who weren't were rejected and others given their chance. There was no particular stigma if pilots were turned down since formation aerobatics is an art on its own. From there we would proceed into stall turns, whereby the leader puts his aircraft into a vertical climb, maintains that attitude until the tell-tale shudder gives warning of the stall, applies rudder and allows the aircraft to cartwheel over into a dive. One had to be careful to catch the aircraft before it really stalled or it would have dropped into a spin. No pilot could maintain formation on another in a spin for both aircraft are literally out of control until remedial action is taken. Aircraft spin in the vertical plane while rotating, and it seems obvious that the thing to do is to pull back on the stick, which is the way to recover from a dive. This indeed is what the early pilots in the RFC used to do, little realizing that such reaction merely tightens the spin. Grave concern was expressed at the number of aeroplanes which spun into the ground and two scientists in particular were instructed to examine the phenomenom – Lindemann and Tizard, both practising pilots. Using mathematical calculations, they decided that the way to get out of a spin was to jam the stick *forward* and kick on opposite rudder shortly afterwards. Lindemann then took up a clapped-out biplane, deliberately put it into a spin, and using his paper calculations got out of it safely. He certainly had more confidence in his mathematical know-how than I would have done!

Then the rookies had to hang onto their leaders' wings in loops, and eventually in rolls which were a mixture of slow rolls and barrel rolls. About eight pilots met the specification and the best of those had to be selected. My flight commanders and myself tested each of these and gave them marks which reduced their number to five, making six when the leader was included. This was sufficient as I wanted to begin displays with four aircraft, three in vic and one in the box behind me. Finally, I decided to select a leader. By right, of course, I could have taken the lead, but seniority was unimportant; for all I knew I might be a shade rusty for such absolute precision flying, so we went through a process of elimination. I flew the team over the dispersal, starting in a low pass and hauling into a loop before running the programme of manoeuvres I had worked out. I put on several performances while my flight commanders, Steve Daniel and Freddie Lister, observed and gave marks. Then Steve had a go while Freddie and I watched from the ground. Finally Freddie took the lead with an imaginative programme. Steve and I agreed from the marking that he was better than we were, so he was made the official team leader. If a display was required, then Steve and I kept in practice in case Freddie was on leave.

This was too much for No 1 squadron, and they decided to form an aerobatic team. If the squadron commander had had any sense, he would have asked for my advice before starting the process, considering that I had formed our team from scratch. We watched their practice runs from the ground and they seemed to be coming along quite well. They used four aircraft too, three in vic and one in the box.

Before flying started on each day, all squadron pilots would assemble in the met briefing room to listen to what the met forecaster had to say. Whatever he said, I would make up my own mind as to weather prospects, and lay down the flying programme for the day accordingly. This particular day would be bright but with gusting winds, strengthening to jet stream force at height, and I decided to fly high level navigation sorties for which pilots would have to lay off quite a lot of degrees to allow for wind drift. If high altitude winds were blowing at 100 mph, which they certainly were on that day, and if a pilot flew to a pin-point on track, not allowing for wind beam on, he would be precisely a hundred miles away from his pin-point after one hour if he didn't allow for drift. I warned my pilots to approach the runway at ten knots above the normal speed to counter low level turbulence, which would be severe.

I drove towards the dispersal and noted to my horror that No 1 squadron's aerobatic team was approaching on a low pass before pulling into a loop to gain height. I knew that disaster was imminent and put my foot on the accelerator heading towards that point. Sure enough, as they pulled up turbulence struck. The Meteor in the box struck the aircraft on the port side of the vic ahead, and dived into the ground in the middle of the airfield. I was first on the scene and found a hole in the ground from which dirty black smoke was beginning to billow. The fire engines arrived and they hosed foam onto the furnace. Tom Prickett raced up, got out of his car and looked at me. I shook my head; they were wasting their time.

Then I spotted a Meteor lurching into land on the grass, and sped to the scene. The pilot was leaning limply over his instrument panel, and all I could do was to race to the hangar and order a light mobile crane to get there pronto, together with a team of men with an assortment of tools. I drove to the hole in the ground and ordered the ambulance to attend on the other Meteor. The remains of the first pilot were beyond medical assistance. After the mechanics had prised open the cockpit canopy with a jemmy and a sledge hammer, I attached the hook of the crane to the second pilot's parachute harness and signalled for the crane operator slowly to lift him out. They lowered him and I released his parachute harness; the medical orderlies strapped him to a stretcher and carted him off to sick quarters in the ambulance. The Meteor had some nasty gashes in the fuselage, and God alone knew how the pilot had managed to land it. More likely than not the aircraft was difficult to control, and the pilot must have been in such a state of shock from the mid-air collision that, after touching down, he passed out in a stupor. It was none of my business, but I was infuriated by this unnecessary tragedy.

No 1 squadron gave up any further attempt to maintain an aerobatic team, but we didn't. We increased the number of aircraft in our team to six. Our efforts were duly rewarded when Fighter Command got downwind of the fact that one of their squadrons had a team of some excellence. We were ordered to fly to the South of France to give a display for the Cannes Flower Festival and stayed there for a week. The French and American Air Forces also had teams, but they were not in our league. M. le Maire presented me with two bottles of Napoleon brandy at the end of our visit. I gave one to the airmen and the other to the pilots. I must have been mad!

CHAPTER 27

But it was not all work and no play at Tangmere. I waited until the next best house after the Station Commander's residence was to become vacant and laid claim to it. During the war it had been converted into the Station Sick Quarters, and was certainly sizeable enough, standing back from the approach road to Tangmere in a large garden. It had more character than Tom Prickett's mansion, being built circa 1926 whereas his was erected in 1938, before which it had been the Station Commander's official residence. RAF quarters are adequately furnished, but with standard issue items, so the interior of one was all too similar to the next. Tom had brightened up his place by putting in a few items of his own, but I decided to go the whole hog. The Clerk of Works' jaw dropped when I told him I wanted the exterior and the interior repainted with my selection of colours, but I had exhausted him in previous battles and he caved in and put his men onto the job. The Barrack Warden jumped up and down when I asked him to remove all RAF issue furniture, save for the third floor which I didn't intend to use. That was impossible; the inventory of furniture went with the house, he explained.

'Bullshit, Bill,' I replied. 'Just pack the stuff in a separate cage in your warehouse where it will be ready for the next occupant.'

When the painting was done, a couple of pantechnicons arrived with my own furniture and pictures. The result was amazing. The place was transformed from a military establishment into a home. Then my wife drove down with our two children and a nanny, and just walked in. We had a full-time batman to help with the cleaning and polishing, so we were home and dry. The garden had gone to seed, so I went to see the head gardener.

'You've got to cut the grass and tend the flower beds in my garden,' I told him.

'And then I go jump over the moon,' was Job's reply. 'If I did any work on your garden, I'd have all the bloody officers' wives on the camp wanting their sodding gardens done.'

'You do the Station Commander's garden,' I pointed out.

'Yes, that's his privilege.'

'Same applies to me,' I told him. 'My garden is over one acre, and regulations say that gardens of that size have to be maintained by Station gardeners.'

'I'll come and measure it,' he said suspiciously.

It was a fraction short of an acre and Job thought he had me cold.

'I'm forming a squadron cricket team for this coming season,' I informed him. 'We'll be playing against neighbouring villages, and using your pitch of course. Make sure it helps the spinners.'

'Gar, I'd love a game of cricket,' he reflected, 'but I ain't so young as I was.'

'I'll make you our travelling umpire if you like,' I suggested. 'We'll carry a barrel of beer to the matches and all that.'

'Gar!' he exclaimed. 'I'm on.'

'How big did you say my garden was?' I enquired.

'Damn near an acre and a half,' he announced without blushing.

Tom Prickett's wife, Betty, was an American from the top drawer. She and my wife soon became good friends, which was a relief to them both. On average, RAF wives can be a funny lot, often lacking social graces, prone to petty jealousies, and all too aware of their husband's rank and status. Thus, if one is married to a Flight Lieutenant, she tends to preen herself in the presence of a Mrs Flying Officer as if she herself outranked the other. On average, this trend gets worse as their men rise in rank and reach the top echelons, and God help her near competitors when one of them becomes Lady Plonk before them. Betty and my wife were above such meaningless trivialities and associated with wives on their merit, not on their husbands' rank. Indeed, Tom rose to the top and finished up as a member of the Air Council, and on his way up Betty became Lady Prickett, which changed her not one whit. But in general, life on a 'married patch' became very tedious, and we tended to make friends with the neighbours who lived more civilized lives. I would say this was the prime reason for my premature retirement. It was difficult for me to stand, and eventually my wife found it impossible, so I asked to be put on the retired list.

But our house provided plenty of room for guests and we had many visitors, which alleviated the strain. One in particular was a cousin, David, with his wife Elizabeth. Before the war he had been a Deb's delight, a considerable roué, and took a commission in the Army when war was impending. He was taken prisoner at Dunkirk, and his volatile temperament revolted, which didn't do his health much good. A friend of his in POW camp was a well known portrait painter and he taught David to paint. Ostensibly they came to stay so that he could paint a portrait of my daughter, then aged about four, and for some odd reason he wanted her to sit on top of a ladder to get the light right. One Saturday the squadron cricket team was due to play against Tom Griffith's side in his local village, and I took David to the Mess at noon and gave him a drink. He was a hard drinker but due to his POW experience his tolerance was low. I was in a hurry so I handed him over to an officer who could drink a camel dry, and they hit the vodka. The bus arrived by my house and I found that we had only ten men for the team. I told the bus to go ahead and I would follow with an eleventh man. I drove to the Mess where David was swaying like a willow tree in a force ten wind.

'Come on,' I said, 'you've got to play cricket.'

'Certainly, old boy. But Patch has got to come too.'

Patch was his fox-terrier.

As we drove to the village in a fold over the Downs, he went to sleep, while Patch licked his face and savoured his breath. We got to the village green, I hauled David out of the car, and he put his arm round my neck and staggered to the hut where he lay down on the grass and went to sleep. Patch also seemed to be a bit pissed. Tom Griffiths, our opponents' captain, lost the toss to me. I elected to bat and decided to open the batting with Ned Kelly. Ned was an Australian Sergeant Pilot, and as Job hadn't yet put the nets up at Tangmere I didn't know how good the pilots were and chose them at random. I had asked Ned if he played cricket and he had admitted he'd heard of the game, which was good enough for me. Off the village green was a lane beyond which was a pub where a crowd of spectators sat swigging beer out of hours, which seemed to be all right as the village copper was in their team.

Tom Griffiths opened the bowling and I hit him for four. His next ball was a slow long-hop which I hit over the lane for six. One of the spectators caught it and Tom appealed.

'Out!' said their umpire.

'What the hell are you talking about?' I enquired. 'That was out of bounds for a six!'

'No it weren't. The boundary ain't the lane, it be the pub. And if you break a window in the pub, you've got to pay for a new window. That's what the rules say.'

'Where are the bloody rules?'

'They're on a board in the pub.'

'All right. But a spectator caught the ball, not one of the team, so I can't be out.'

'It says in the rules that the team consists of the villagers of Charlbury, not just the men in the field. Pity you didn't read the rules, Sir.'

I threw a bucket of water over David's head when he was due to bat last man in. He blindly swept the first three balls for four apiece, and on the next delivery he sat on his wicket and went to sleep. Ned made fifty not out, and would have made 500 if anyone had been able to stay with him.

We went out to field and I put David at long leg where he lay down with Patch squatting alongside him. I bowled at Tom Griffiths who deflected it to leg for a certain four. Patch got up and intercepted the ball and roared back to the wicket keeper with the ball in his mouth.

'That's not fair!' Tom, who hadn't bothered to start running, yelled. 'You can't have a bloody dog as a fielder.'

'Yes you can, Tom,' I replied. 'It's in the rules isn't it, Job?'

'Course it's in the rules,' he stated. 'I'm surprised at you, Tom Griffiths. You should know the rules you should.'

'Where are the bloody rules?' Tom enquired. 'I've never seen them.'

'They are on the board in my squadron dispersal hut,' I informed him.

'But I'm not allowed on the bloody airfield!' he protested, 'so how can I have read the rules?'

'The rules say that players of both sides should familiarize themselves with the rules before play begins,' I told him. 'So that's your bloody fault.'

Tom went for a second run next ball, but Patch was too quick for him, and handed the ball to the keeper who swept the bails off.

'Out!' Job, who was thoroughly enjoying himself, announced.

They were all out for ten. Ned did most of the damage with his chinamen.

Then we opened the keg of beer and David came to with a start.

'God, I feel like a drink,' he said.

'You even look like a drink,' I informed him.

We had an enjoyable season playing in the charming villages nestling in the Downs. But then came squash, and I captained the Station Officers' team. We held our own against various clubs, but there was one occasion I prefer to forget. Billy Griffiths had played a lot of cricket for some county like Surrey, also, I believe for England. Being an international cricketer obviously gave him an excellent eye for squash. He was captain of one of the club teams we came across and we played each other. I didn't score a point. This impressed on me the vast difference between a good average club player and a good county, or country, player. In the latter category, the eye is that much keener and the reactions that much quicker. Such people quite often, though not invariably, make good fighter pilots. In faraway 1941 a golfer of international repute joined No 66 squadron, by name Laddie Lucas. He couldn't fly for toffee because he was too inexperienced, but I realized his potential and made him a flight commander as soon as possible. I was right; he went to Malta and made a great name for himself.

CHAPTER 28

Tom Prickett and I became firm friends, although things remained on a formal level in working routine. He had a great knack for solving difficult problems without fussing unduly. For example, it became apparent that my predecessor, now Officer i/c Flying, was harassing my flight commanders when I took leave, or went off on courses. He made no such attempt when I was in the chair, and all bloody hell would have been let loose if he had. But this put my senior flight commander in an intolerable position, because I formally handed command over to him before I went away. There was no point in having it out with Tony Brown because he would have dodged the issue, so I wrote a personal letter to Tom explaining the circumstances, in order that he could tactfully intervene in my absence. Things weren't made any easier since Tony, although of the same rank, was senior to me. Nothing happened until one Saturday a month later, when Tom invited me to take him for a drive round the airfield in my private car, on the pretext that he wanted to listen to the boat-race on the car radio without domestic interference. We listened to the boat-race and Cambridge won, then he came to the point.

'I've been thinking about the Tony Brown problem, and the situation of your flight commanders,' he said. 'Do you know what I propose to do about it?'

'Yes, Sir,' I replied.

He raised his eyebrows.

'What am I going to do about it then?' he enquired.

'Nothing,' I said.

'You must be a bloody mind reader.'

In fact, he must have done something about it – dropped a hint perhaps. Anyway, my flight commanders suffered no more interference.

As my wife and I knew more of the 'County' folk living around Tangmere than the Pricketts, I thought I should introduce them into this closed circuit. My wife had been in touch with such people whom she had met during and shortly after the war, and we were often invited to take drinks off them or whatever. When we returned their hospitality in our little mansion, I always tried to get Tom and Betty Prickett along to meet them. It is useful for a Station Commander to get to know the local gentry, and in turn the couple certainly had the social graces likely to add kudos to the good name of the RAF. For various reasons the RAF is not popular with the 'upper crust', whose members never understand the nomenclature of various ranks. They don't know the difference between a Flight Lieutenant and an Air Vice Marshal, and who can blame them.

The most splendid opportunity arose when Olive Snell telephoned my wife and told her that Ebenezer Pike had completed the rehabilitation of their house after its occupation by troops, and she was laying on a house-warming party. My wife said we would be delighted to attend and asked if we could bring two friends along. A card duly arrived inviting us with two friends along for a ball and buffet. I had warned Tom to keep that date clear from other engagements, and the four of us set forth, Tom and I in black ties, and the ladies looking a million in long dresses. The house was a Palladian sort of mansion standing half-way up the Downs between Chichester and Arundel, with a few million quid's worth of Rolls-Royces parked outside. Candle-lit chandeliers glittered on ceilings embossed and picked out in gilt, and the reception rooms were big enough for a pair of rugby teams to have a match. Everyone who was anyone was there, and I calculated that if I could spirit away just five per cent of the tiaras and diamond necklaces, I could move to the Bahamas with my own troupe of dancing girls. Two leading London dance bands took it in turn to provide the music; one was the great Ambrose and his Mayfair band. A river of champagne flowed, and white-gloved flunkeys were there to wipe the sweat from your brow. The buffet was out of this world. There were enough plovers eggs and caviare to keep a small country going for a couple of days. Betty was a sophisticated American, but she could never have viewed a scene like this before.

The cabaret was equally stupendous. The cream of entertainers had come down, probably for the party not for a fee. Noël Coward sang pornographic songs; Gertrude Lawrence did her stuff; Joyce Grenfell ran through some of her monologues; and heaven knows who did heaven knows what. Then for those more culturally inclined a buxom opera singer burst into a cantata. At this point I elbowed Tom in the ribs; we exited from a casement door onto the terrace, sat down and savoured our cigars. The decibels from the cacophonous cantata hardly penetrated the peace of the night and all was well with the world. Clearly, the Duke of Richmond couldn't stand the row either and I saw him pacing up and down in the half light. I grabbed Tom by the arm and introduced them to each other. The long term effect of this meeting came to fruition a couple of decades later. When Tom left the RAF covered in accolades, Freddy Richmond invited him to become a member of the Board of the Goodwood Estates.

On the other side of the coin, RAF Officers Messes also had a biannual ball, and the Messes themselves provided excellent facilities. The dining hall at Tangmere, with its parquet floor and the raised stage which contained the band, gave plenty of room for dancing and a buffet. The furniture in the ante-room was rearranged, and it was the place to sit or stand and drink. Stations could often produce quite good dance bands comprised of NCOs and airmen, who were togged up in evening dress for the occasion; if not, outside bands were hired for the purpose. Officers' wives normally did the flower arranging; the Mess was decorated with a canopy and fairy lights leading to the entrance doors; and a powder-room was made available for the ladies. Percy and his cooks could always be relied on to produce an excellent buffet. Tables were arranged so that officers and their wives could make up parties of six, but the Station Commander had a larger table because he had to host VIP guests. He had to put up some of them in his house, which was often a grim chore, and my wife and I would ask personal friends to come down and stay. If bedroom accommodation in Tom's house was likely to overspill, he would ask us to take on some of the official guests which we found blindingly boring. The dress was black tie for male civilians, Mess wear for those officers who had the kit, a black tie with a white shirt under best uniform for those who didn't, and long evening dresses for the ladies.

We duly laid on a ball which finished up a great success, having begun on a note of the utmost hilarity. The story illustrates the attitudes of all too many wives of senior RAF officers. Official guests were to assemble in Tom's house before going to the Mess, to take drinks and relax. He asked us to get there early to help break the ice. The Air Officer Commanding No 11 Group and his wife were staying with him for the night. The Duke and Duchess of Richmond had been invited since he was not only an honorary member of the Mess but a distinguished neighbour. They slipped into the drawing-room unobtrusively through a side door, and my wife and I button-holed them while Tom and Betty engaged the other guests. Some time elapsed, and Tom was looking anxiously at his watch, before the AOC and his wife decided to make a grand entry. Tom's house steward flung open the double doors leading into the drawing room, the AOC and his missis entered and stood motionless, waiting for all and sundry to come to a breathless hush. I saw them from the corner of my eye and went on talking to Freddy about racing cars. No one else took a blind bit of notice of them except Tom who was on the *qui vive*. He greeted them and led them into the middle of the common throng. He nudged Betty in the ribs, and she tackled the disdainful Mrs AOC.

But the belly-splitting guffaw came when Mrs AOC dragged Betty into a corner.

'Who,' she demanded to know, 'is that *dreadful* man over there?' She nodded in Freddy's direction.

'Why, he's the Duke of Richmond,' Betty informed her.

'There's no such person as the Duke of Richmond,' she stated with authority, even though the title dates back to the reign of Charles II. 'The man is an imposter. You should call the police!'

Betty is a tough hombre; she has to be to keep Tom

under control. Her normal speech is Bostonian, near-English, but on this occasion she put on a broad American drawl.

'Well, I don't know about what you say,' she said, 'but whatever it is he is *your* Dook, not mine.'

By contrast, when we arrived at the Mess, Freddy Richmond took my wife by the arm and led her into the bar, which was a noisy, seething mass.

'Cor blimey!' he said, wiping his forehead. 'Don't harf strike warm don't it.'

CHAPTER 29

In the shooting season I taught Tom the arts of 'inspecting the airfield' at dusk. We would lurch along in a jeep, headlights blazing, one of us driving and the other wielding a shot-gun. Hares always gave us a good run, although I have long given up shooting them, but rabbits for the dogs were easy meat. We flushed out coveys of partridge quite often, and the odd pheasant took off in range. But we shot strictly for the pot and never indulged in any massacres. We also partnered each other at tennis on Sunday mornings, playing against neighbours and finishing up with cool drinks of Pimms. Tom would rush up and down like a bull in a china shop, heaving and puffing and bellowing curses if he made a balls of things. It was all most enjoyable.

Wednesday afternoons was set aside for organized games for those not on essential duty and, cricket apart, organized games such as rugby, soccer and athletics gave me a pain in the neck. Quite rightly, Tom felt it his duty to show some enthusiasm *pour encourager les autres*, and he used to referee rugby matches. I normally flight-tested aeroplanes in need on Wednesdays, because I hold the view that the best way to keep fit for flying was to fly. An avid PT Staff Officer came down one day in an attempt to expand his little empire, and said it was essential that I should get my pilots doing physical jerks before breakfast. I persuaded him to climb into the back seat of a Meteor Mk 7, blacked him out at 3 gee and kept him blacked out for some time. He was sick of course, and when we landed I told him he was unfit for flying, and that pilots had to have a gee tolerance of four and a half gee. He drove away in a cloud of dust muttering that he had joined the Air Force to train people in physical jerks, not to fly in bleeding aeroplanes. The ground branches are always screwed up and get immersed in their parochial work to the extent that they don't realize, whether they are cooks or clerks, that their main purpose in the RAF is to keep the aircraft flying, whether directly or indirectly.

However, I had been working out a scheme in collaboration with the Station Engineer Officer whereby I would be able to produce smoke from a Meteor at will. Screwed under the bellies of the Meteors were large, streamlined overload fuel tanks containing 180 gallons of kerosene. We called engineer officers plumbers, and our plumber conferred with scientists from the nearest Shell depot, and it was decided that a particular compound of chemicals, if exposed to the air in a high wind, would vaporize and turn into smoke. The plumber and his fitters devised a Heath Robinson gadget whereby chemicals would be released from the overload tank to provide white smoke, which would be cut off when the handle was pulled back. On Wednesday afternoon when Tom was doing his stuff on the rugby field, we topped up the tank with chemicals, and I took off. I made a high speed run towards the airfield, and pulled the handle. I shut it down, climbed and looked over my shoulder. Sure enough there was a thick pall of white smoke indicating my flight path. I climbed to 20,000 feet and decided to muck up Tom's rugby match. I came down in a high speed dive and pulled the handle as I just missed the rugby posts. I climbed away and noted that the pitch was covered in dense white smoke. I climbed again, got up speed, dived on the pitch and did four upward charlies, leaving the handle open. Before I landed I gave a performance of low level aerobatics using smoke.

I taxied in and the plumber was there to meet me. He had a quick look at the Meteor as I was climbing out of the cockpit.

'Good show!' I said. 'It worked fine.'

'No it bloody well didn't,' he groaned. 'The aircraft is a write-off.'

There were holes in the stressed skin of the fuselage and the tail fin was on the point of dropping off. The chemicals had eroded the metal, and if I had kept her aloft for another five minutes she would have fallen to bits. However, I sent a report to the boffins at Farnborough who took an interest in R & D, hence the Red Arrows and their red, white and blue smoke. Hence the Red Arrows, as a matter of fact, because of the efforts made in establishing No 43 squadron's aerobatic team. Of course, their pilots do nothing else except Fred Carno circus performances, but we did it in our spare time, while remaining strictly operational.

The two seater Meteor Mk 7 was a useful toy. A lot of VIPs visited the squadron, and the Adjutant kept a visitor's book for mundane folk, whereas I kept one for distinguished visitors which soon filled with signatures and was sent to the squadron archive. The Chief of the Air Staff, Sir John Slessor, came to see us and he had never flown in a jet, so I gave him a flip much to his satisfaction. He suffered from infantile paralysis at a tender age which left him with a game leg. But he flew in World War I. We found it much more difficult getting him into the back seat of a Meteor than it would have been in a clapped-out Sopwith one-and-a-half strutter.

Parties of officers and men from the Army and Navy came to see us to try and pick up a little of the mystique surrounding flying. I wasn't going to allow the Meteor Mk 7 to be overflown because we only had one, so on such occasions they had to draw lots as to who was going to be given a ride, and most of those who were successful wished they hadn't been. Most of them were terrified at the prospect. If the flight commanders were going to take them up, I warned them to fly it nice and easy, as I did myself. I always gave them a running commentary so as not to alarm them. The patter went something like this:

'The canopy is locked and sealed, your oxygen is flowing. I am about to start the engines. Am now opening the throttles to taxi to the runway. Lined up for take off, applying brakes and giving her full throttle. Releasing brakes for take off, you will feel a thump in your back. We are airborne, retracting undercarriage. Climbing to 20,000 feet, press your nose and puff to balance your eardrums. Turning port over the sea, heading for Brighton. Do you feel like any aerobatics? OK, we'll do a couple of rolls. Opening throttles again and making easy turn over Brighton, you will be pushed back into your seat. Heading for Tangmere, ground speed 500 mph. Throttling back and extending the dive brakes prior to descent, you will feel the aircraft shuddering. Descending, press your nose and puff. Joining circuit to land, applying fifteen degrees of flap. Final turn, putting down full flap. Undercarriage going down, you will hear a thump. Stalling her onto the runway.'

That took about fifteen minutes and I would keep the engines running while the next 'volunteer' was strapped in, and repeat the procedure. We could cram in four flights without stopping the engines. People varied widely in their reactions. I took up four Royal Marines one day, the first of whom was a Sergeant. Yes he wanted to aerobat. That was fun, could he have some more? I flew back to base looping, rolling, stall turning and flick rolling all the way. He gave me a grin and the thumbs up sign as he climbed out of the cockpit. The last man in was a Captain. No, he didn't want any aerobatics. He was violently sick when he got out. It was nerves, of course. If the air had been turbulent there would have been some excuse, but it was smooth as a virgin's bottom.

My brother came to stay, and he was an Army officer. He is the elder by three years, and a Mr bloody know-all to boot. Before I started flying, I bought a book *Teach Yourself to Fly*, and very good it was too. He read it and began to impress on me actual flying techniques. When I was an *ab initio* trainee, he would write explaining how to slow roll, and all that sort of garbage. He had visited me at various Stations where I gave him the occasional flip in a light training aeroplane, nothing vicious, and he had never seen a jet before, so I decided to put the wind up him. We arrived over the Isle of Wight at 40,000 feet, and went into a rolling dive; half-way down I slammed out the dive brakes without warning, and he thought the wings were falling off as she juddered ferociously at such high speed. I almost clipped the Needles and regained height doing upward charlies on the way, let her run out of airspeed and corrected her as she hit the spin. After a little more cavorting, I settled down at 400 knots, 250 feet above the sea, heading for Selsey Bill.

He had remained silent thus far; perhaps he was speechless. But when I had settled on course, I raised my hands above my head so he could see them, and said over the intercom – 'You are in control.' That immediately aroused him.

'Are you bloody mad?' he screeched. 'I can't fly this sodding aircraft.'

'You always told me you could fly an aeroplane without flying an aeroplane, so now's your chance. Just keep her straight and level. Whoops, you're putting on too much right aileron, better correct it.'

'I'm not touching the bloody stick!' he yelled. Nor was he; I had nudged the stick with my knee. I nudged it back.

'That very good,' I said. 'Now try a slight dive.'

'I'm buggered if I'm going to touch anything,' he cursed. 'And we're nearly in the sea already.'

'Well, you'd better pull back a bit because you'll have us in the sea all right. Don't be so ham-fisted.' I had used my knee again.

'Put your hand on the sodding controls!' he shrieked, 'and get us out of this.'

'You can see I'm not touching the controls. My hands are above my head. It's you who are buggering up the controls. Now take a grip of yourself.'

I kept up the agony for as long as was prudent, and then took control. But as a finale, I let the main wheels touch the runway, slammed open the throttles and took off again.

'There's something wrong,' I said. 'She won't land. You must have jammed the controls.'

'I haven't put a finger on the bloody controls,' he protested.

'Don't worry. I'll gain a bit of height, then we'll bale out.'

'I don't know how to sodding well bale out!'

'That's OK. I'll tell you on the way down.'

CHAPTER 30

We re-equipped with Meteors Mk 8, which had a marginally superior performance and longer engine nacelles more in proportion. You couldn't disguise the fact that it was a Meteor – they all looked like dead turkeys, but they were new aircraft and our Mks 4 had flown hundreds of hours by now. The Gloster Aircraft Company only produced two decent aircraft in their history, the Gauntlet and the Gladiator, both of which were biplanes. Their 'revolutionary' Javelin which came into squadron service in the 1950s should have been put in the Chamber of Horrors.

Someone from the City Hall contacted me one day with a pleasant surprise. During the war a fund had been raised by the citizens of Chichester for the welfare of members of No 43 squadron. It hadn't been distributed because 43 was all over the place in the war, so would I come and collect a cheque for about £500. Would I not! In liaison with Council officials I laid on a PR operation of some magnitude. On an agreed Saturday morning the squadron would march from the top of East Street to the City Hall. My flight commanders and I would enter the Mayor's parlour to receive the cheque, then he would take the salute when we shoved off. My Flight Sergeant Discip was fairly useless, but at least he could give the airmen some marching drill. I called on the Station Warrant Officer to exercise the officers in sword drill. I also liaised with the Police.

On the selected day a convoy of cars and buses stopped beyond East Street and we formed up with me at the head, the adjutant behind and the two flight commanders leading their flights. The Police cleared the streets which were smothered with holiday-makers, and we had to make an awkward turn round the old Cross in the centre of the city. We came to a halt outside the City Hall, the men marched on and got out of the way and I took the flight commanders to the Mayor's hide-out. I'd warned the Press and they took pictures of the Mayor handing over the cheque after he had given us some rather bad sherry. He quite liked a bit of PR too. Then we rejoined the troops, marched past the Mayor with swords dipped, got back to the buses and rode back to Tangmere. I wrote to the Mayor thanking him and the citizens for the cheque, and also for making the squadron a Freeman of the City. He didn't know what the hell I was talking about, but a military unit can only march through a city with bayonets fixed if it is a Freeman. I deliberately ordered fixed bayonets, so he had no option except to make No 43 a Freeman! Poor old No 1 squadron's morale sank to its nadir after this coup.

During the silly summer season we were in great demand to overfly various air shows and military tattoos in the Southern and Home counties. In a squadron formation at my allotted time, we would make a low pass over the spectators, vanish and return in different sorts of formation. On our last pass we would break it up in split-arse fashion, disappear and reform when out of sight. There was always demand for the aerobatic team, and I would get to the venue ahead of time and make a running commentary over the tannoys. Fighter leaders should be expert broadcasters since they constantly transmit instructions in the air to their pilots, so commentaries were no skin off my nose. When I was on the hot seat at HQ 11 Group, we had to lay on the biggest flypast in RAF history as a salute to the Queen after her Coronation. All RAF Commands produced aircraft for the purpose, 615 in all.

The planning had to be precise, aircraft based as far afield as Pembroke Dock, Londonderry to Kinloss in the north of Scotland had to be fed into the aerial parade. We also had to teach Bomber Command how to fly in close formation, a seemingly impossible task. The impossible took a little time and a lot of anguish, but on the day the mean error in the timing of the formations was ten seconds. I did the commentary, and when the thing was over my AOC, my SASO and myself took ourselves to a mental home to recuperate from our nervous breakdowns. I also did the commentary on the Golden Jubilee of the formation of the RAE Farnborough, attended by Princess Margaret. A Hunter dived into the ground shortly after take off, and I pretended not to notice, so people were practically unaware of the tragedy. I've done a lot of broadcasting on radio and TV, but I never suffered from butterflies in the tummy because of my long apprenticeship.

Such were the demands for displays that I changed the working routine as we were always wanted on Saturdays. I decided to work the squadron on Saturdays and stand it down on Mondays in lieu. This wasn't particularly satisfactory, so after a time I pointed out that HQFC had about fifty fighter squadrons they could use, not just No 43, and if the other buggers couldn't form their own aerobatic teams then I would go along and teach them. They didn't seem to take the hint, so I warned them that I was having trouble with my serviceability rate. When the next request came along, I sent a signal regretting that I didn't have any serviceable aircraft. I didn't mind if they sent down an engineer officer to check this out, because my skilled fitters could have put all the aircraft unserviceable in half an hour in such a way that no outsider would ever discover the reason why. Orders were sent to the squadrons instructing them to form aerobatic teams, but I put the boot in again by suggesting that this was a terrible waste of resources. Fighter pilots were supposed to be training for war, not to emulate trapeze artistes. Formation aerobatics was no counter to being shot up the backside by a Soviet MiG. We had done it on the cheap, and managed to maintain our operational training programme at the same time, and we had only done it because it was a great squadron tradition. Most squadrons did not have formation aerobatics in their pedigrees. I estimated the flying hours and additional man hours we expended on the training programme, suggested that the figure should be doubled in the case of most other squadrons who wouldn't know how to do it on the cheap, and then mutiplied by the number of squadrons in the Command. It was positively an astronomical total on non-essential training. The solution was to form a specialist unit doing nothing else but formation aerobatics, preferably outside Fighter Command. As always, it took time before the new idea was accepted, but finally the Red Arrows were formed in Flying Training Command. Then the RAF had its own flying circus, free to travel to international air displays.

Overflying London in massed formations was a tricky operation. Assuming ten squadrons were utilized, each would have to arrive over the lead-in point, which was somewhere like Southend Pier, at a precise time and altitude, at a prearranged speed. When I say precise I mean exactly that, give or take five seconds at most. The practice was that each squadron would fly thirty seconds behind the one ahead, which put it in visual range. If one arrived over the lead-in point thirty seconds late, it would probably collide with the squadron which was supposed to be behind it on the run into London.

I remember one mid-air collision when my old friend Bob Yule was killed. He took command of No 66 squadron about a year after I left when it was based at

Warmwell in Dorset. It was a turbulent day and his wingman collided with his Meteor. He made a direct hit on Woolwich Arsenal and his wingman managed to go up in his rocket ejection seat.

Overflying London was turbulent anyway, even on a calm day. The squadron behind the leader would fly below to avoid the slipstream, the next one behind would fly at the same height as the leader and so on along the line. But to take it to its extreme, if you were the tail end charlie at the end of the mass, as I once was, the air was awash with the turbulence of a hundred aircraft ahead. I had to wrestle with the controls, and those maintaining close formation on me would have had a hell of a job to retain control, but I kept the squadron in loose formation and tightened it up as we neared the target – usually Buckingham Palace.

There is never a dull moment when commanding an active fighter squadron. I spent a lot of time in the ATC tower watching the controllers at work, ensuring that they were handling my pilots in correct fashion, giving them hints and tips to correct their procedures if they were making a hash of things. Indeed I would take them up in the back of a Meteor Mk 7 and show them how their colleagues got things right or wrong from the receiving end. The ATC caravan at the upwing end of the runway was also a good vantage point from which to observe my pilots take off and land, when I would sharpen them up if necessary. I regularly visited the maintenance hangar where our fitters and mechanics did the major work on the aircraft, and encouraged the pilots to do likewise. These chaps worked in a kind of garage atmosphere and it was important to remind them they were part of a front line squadron. I would arrange cross-postings so that personnel working on the line would get some hangar experience, and those on more serious inspections could get some time on the line. This was double-edged for the maintenance men worked in a relatively cosy hangar, and didn't take too kindly to doing their stint in the rain and snow. The welfare of the men and NCOs was uppermost, and I had to advise people even on such things as marriage guidance. One of the main reasons I enjoyed the job of squadron commander was that it kept one in close touch with the NCOs and men, even though one was the local Napoleon. Of course I had to hand out summary justice if the rules were broken for reasons of stupidity or a criminal mind; you can't run a disciplined force in any other way. But provided you were seen to be just and fair, the miscreants hardly held it against you. Like any other institutions the RAF has a criminal element, and the severity of their punishment rose according to their previous convictions. Some of them ended up in military prisons at places like Shepton Mallet and Colchester where their treatment was less than amusing.

Officers and NCOs had to be carefully assessed, so did airmen which was the job of their SNCOs and flight commanders. Promotion depended to some extent on seniority, but enthusiasts could gain accelerated promotion by proving their mettle on the job. Officers on short-service commissions would be recommended for regular commissions if they met the standards, and regular officers would benefit from improving their performance. Confidential report forms demanded that I assessed officers in great detail, from the quality of their intellect, the manner in which they dressed, their qualities of leadership, their pilot ability to their social graces and so on. This didn't mean that I had to hide under their beds at night, nor follow them around with a magnifying glass, but whether they knew it or not they were always under observation. After all, today's junior officers, or some of them, become tomorrow's senior officers in due course.

What one had to avoid was favouritism: you had to be as impartial as a judge – which is what you were. Officers in the Army or Navy know the contents of their confidential reports, indeed in the Army they have to read and initial them. Officers in the RAF are not allowed to know anything about what has been written which is grossly unfair. I know of a number of cases where reporting officers took the view that if they gave a true indication of a bright chap's performance, he might overtake them in the promotion stakes in the long run. All too many reporting officers felt insecure and were positively jealous of a rising star, and they would vent their ids by writing petty and vindictive assessments. With my mercurial temperament, unorthodox methods, and contempt for stupid regulations, more orthodox reporting officers simply did not understand me; but on the other hand sage judges such as Tom Prickett, and I could mention other famous names, understood me very well. There were supposed to be safeguards written into the system but they simply don't work, yet the RAF still refuses officers the right to see their confidential reports, and for the wrong reasons.

With experience it is not too difficult to assess officers fairly and squarely. An accurate assessment can make all the difference to their careers. One example was the case of a newly-joined short-service commissioned officer who joined The Fighting Cocks at the age of twenty-one. Previously he had been a cub reporter on his local newspaper, and was mature beyond his years. He was personable, amusing, took his work seriously, was good at handling the airmen, and in a short time was found worthy of being selected for the aerobatic team. I spotted a man with a high potential and after a few months decided to write him up for a permanent commission. At about which moment he came to see me and formally requested permission to get married. Before the war, officers were supposed to remain 'married' to the Service until they were twenty-five, and were given a black mark if they broke the rule. In any case they had to ask formal permission of their Commanding Officer to get married.

'As a matter of fact, old boy,' I said. 'I'm thinking of putting you up for a regular commission. If I do so, I'll have to mention the fact that you intend to get married which will certainly bar your chances. I'd hang on for a while if I were you.'

'That's good of you, Sir, but I intend to get married come hell or high water. Bugger a regular commission. And I haven't put her in pod, if that's what you're thinking!'

I tried to talk him out of it, but he remained adamant, so I said I would write him up anyway though his chances would now be slim. Then I rang up Tom Prickett, explained the situation and suggested he waited for my recommendation before seeing the guy. He did, and tried to talk him out of it, but he wouldn't budge. Before long this chap came to see me again in an excited state and told me he had been instructed to be interviewed by the C-in-C. I rubbed a little salt in the wound.

'The C-in-C is Air Marshal Sir Basil Embry,' I explained. 'He wears four DSOs, is the toughest hombre on earth, and he was shot down over occupied Europe in a light bomber early in the war. He hid up in a manure heap for twenty-four hours, breathing through a straw, and three German soldiers started to prod his manure heap with bayonets. He burst out of the shit, threw them to the ground, killed one by booting his head in, and jumped on the faces of the other two and managed to escape to Britain. The Germans put a price on his head. By then he was an Air Commodore, but he continued to overfly Germany in Mosquitoes dressed in the rank of Wing

Commander, although he knew that this wouldn't fool the Hun. He knows you intend to get married out of turn, and he'll probably chuck you out of the window for being bloody pig-headed. The best of British luck.'

He left all pale and shaking. On his return he reported to me in a relaxed state.

'How did you get on?'

'Well, Sir, all he said to me was that he noted I intended to get married under age and that he ought to tear up your recommendation. However, as he had confidence in you and Wing Commander Prickett, he would pass me.'

After some distinguished senior appointments, that chap is now an Air Chief Marshal, and it is not improbable that he will finish up as CAS. Sometimes you pick 'em, sometimes you don't. I happened to pick a good 'un.

CHAPTER 31

Tom arrived in my office one day looking gloomy. He slumped in a chair and looked at me.

'I've got bad news,' he said. 'Don't explode in my face.'

'What? Am I in the shit again?'

'That's a permanent condition. You've got to move your squadron to Leuchars.'

Leuchars is an RAF Station near St Andrews in the Kingdom of Fife.

'Why? Do they want fighter cover over Balmoral?'

'Don't be bloody silly. No 43 squadron is to redeploy permanently from Tangmere to Leuchars.'

Whereupon I did explode: I'd never heard such nonsense. No 43 belonged to Tangmere. Even the sodding RAF couldn't be as stupid as that. What about the air defence of London? How the hell could I change our squadron song – 'We are the Fighting Forty-three. We come from Sussex by the sea.' What about traditional values? What about our legacy as a Freeman of Chichester? He let me rant on until I was exhausted.

'I've told them all that,' he said. 'They say the air threat now comes from the north-east, and they want you up there to sharpen things up a bit. You've got to move in a month.'

'I can't sharpen things up with a squadron of clapped-out Meteors!'

'They are arranging for No 43 to be the first squadron to be equipped with the new Hunter. They want you to get acclimatized first.'

'The bloody Hunter is subsonic. Why don't they buy a squadron of Soviet MiG 15s?'

'For God's sake stop talking balls. Come along to the Mess and I'll buy you a drink. Then you can start thinking about the move.'

I was already thinking about the move, but first I had to try and stop it. I immediately started off a powerful lobby with names including MRAF Lord Douglas and Lord Balfour of Inchrye who had been Under Secretary of State at the Air Ministry from 1938 to 1944. Douglas had formed No 43 and Balfour had twice been a flight commander. There were many other distinguished senior officers who had served with the squadron. But Basil Embry was a hard nut and he wouldn't be shifted despite the pressure.

The facts of life soon struck me when Dusty Miller came to see me.

'What the hell do you want?' I snarled. 'I'm busy.'

'Compassionate reasons, Sir. I hear the squadron is moving to Leuchars.'

'That's supposed to be a secret,' I hissed.

'And so it is. But I happen to know a chap in the decoding section of the signals traffic department.'

'I'll put you on a charge under the Official Secrets Act. What do you want?'

'It's my grandmother the noo. She's dying in Dundee.'

'What's that got to do with me? I didn't put any whisky in her tea.'

'I'd like to comfort the old lady on her death-bed. Dundee's no distance from Leuchars. You get to the Tay ten miles away, and take a ferry across. On compassionate grounds, I demand to be posted to 43 squadron.'

'You haven't got a grandmother, you never had a mother, you weren't born you just materialized. But you're on, I'll be needing you. Wait a week until you get formal notification.'

That, at least, was one bonus point.

I had in my existing Flight Sergeant Discip and asked him if he wanted to come with us to Leuchars or stay at Tangmere. As I expected, his grandmother was dying in Portsmouth. Then I asked Tom Prickett if he would agree to a notice being put in Station Daily Orders informing NCOs and men who had good reason to be posted to Scotland to apply to me, when their requests would be considered. Similarly, No 43 personnel who preferred not to move to Leuchars could apply to be cross-posted to No 1 squadron. I was embarrassed at the flood of applicants who wanted to join us, and the very few who wanted to stay behind. Cross-postings were arranged as soon as applicants had been interviewed. It was a sensible policy which was why Tom agreed, but I had to reject most of the applicants who wanted to join us, because members of the squadron, even the bad 'uns, had a right to stay with it.

There was a lot of planning necessary. A special passenger-cum-goods train had to be laid on for loading to commence a week before we moved. Freddie Lister flew up to Leuchars on a forward recce to sort out our hangar and officers rooms in the Mess, and he took with him Dusty Miller to inspect the airmen's barrack block and Sergeants Mess accommodation. Freddie said the ATC procedures stank, and Dusty said the barrack block was a bloody shambles. Leuchars was sleepily unaware of what was going to hit them, which was why we were being sent there, I suppose.

I decided to lay on a theatrical show for all Station personnel in the cinema, for there was a lot of talent among the officers and men. Rehearsals began in the evenings with immediate effect, and suitable costumes were hired from a local theatrical costumier. So was a bagpipe for Dusty Miller to play; he said he could only play after consuming a bottle of whisky, and I told him he would get one on the day but meanwhile he was to practise laments and dirges. A guest night would be held in our honour and I packed the guest list with senior ex-43 officers who would be sure to indicate their disapproval of the redeployment.

Leuchars had been a Coastal Command Station, and the hangars were large enough to house all the aircraft overnight. The offices were in brick annexes attached to the hangar – such luxuries I had never met before. I studied the weather patterns, and the weather factor was good save for one possibly fatal aspect. Weather from the west was lifted by the mountains and could be relied on. But with an easterly or nor'easterly drift, even in high pressure conditions, fog hung over the cold North Sea and could drift in with alarming velocity – they called this the haar. Diversion bases were scarce and there was all too much mountainous terrain. Clearly, in calm conditions, or if easterlies prevailed, I would have to keep a hawk-like eye on the weather. Coastal Stations were used to handling long-range aircraft with plenty of fuel in reserve for diversions. To be effective, I would have to give priority to sharpening up ATC procedures to cope with fighters approaching to land with only five minutes' fuel left in the tanks; they needed enough to overshoot and attempt another landing.

In the event my predictions proved to be correct. After all but strangling the Senior Air Traffic Control Officer and abusing his controllers, I gave him a flip in a Meteor Mk 7 to show him what I meant. Slowly, oh so slowly, I caught the monkey, but it took a bit of doing. But that was in the future.

While at Tangmere, the flying programme was slowed down and attention paid to getting all the aircraft serviceable. Then they were cleaned and polished ready for their nice big all-weather hangar. The squadron silver was polished once again; there were far more items than in No 1 squadron's impressive collection. That would first decorate the table at our guest night, then it would be taken to Leuchars under surveillance of a couple of officers. In the dining hall hung a World War I propeller, the property of No 43 squadron. It had hung there since the squadron was reformed in 1926, in peace and war. Tangmere wouldn't be Tangmere without that propeller, and Leuchars didn't deserve it. I decided to hang it in my office after we arrived.

We put on our theatrical show which was surprisingly good, and it included satirical sketches pulling the legs of No 1 squadron and of Tom Prickett and his Station officers. Of course there were dancing 'girls' and that sort of jazz. I gave a speech and Tom did likewise wishing us Godspeed. In due time the special train was loaded day after day, and the fighting cocks were allocated a whole covered wagon for their coop, whereas Cockie would be put in a small one. A couple of airmen were detailed to feed and water them when the train journey was imminent. Dusty ensured that the barrack block was licked into shape, while we waited for Doomsday.

CHAPTER 32

On the day of the guest night Rupert Leigh and his wife arrived for tea, and it was clear that he was aware that I was feeling particularly venomous at having to remove No 43 from Tangmere. He dropped the hint that the senior ranks on the Station would shortly be upgraded, making Tom a Group Captain and the Officer i/c Flying a Wing Commander. He wafted the notion that I was a candidate for the i/c Flying job, but if I hit the C-in-C between the eyes, small hope that I would get it. I said I didn't give a bugger about getting the flying job. I was OC No 43 Squadron, and as it had been decided to redeploy it, I intended to see it settled in and stay with it until my time was up. He looked anxious. We got togged up, had a drink and walked to the Mess which was only a couple of hundred yards away.

The PMC was No 1 squadron's CO and he greeted us. We grabbed drinks off a wine waiter as Tom Prickett arrived, followed in turn by squadron and Station officers, then came the guests. Paddy, the Mess Steward, muttered in Tom's ear, and he shoved off to fetch the C-in-C who had just landed. Basil Embry wasn't particularly tall but he was as erect as a ramrod. His face was stern, not prone to smiling, and his grey/blue eyes withered your skull with a laser-like penetration. He looked like he was – a man of steel, not someone to cross swords with. He had a habit of closing on someone he was talking to until his face almost collided with yours, leaving two alternatives: either to back away until you hit the wall, or to stand firm until his hot breath fanned your face. I preferred to stand firm. He was by no means a bully, but what he said certainly went – or else.

Paddy announced that dinner was served and we all trooped into the dining-hall, glittering with No 43 squadron's silver and flickering candelabra. Embry was placed on the right of the PMC, Tom sat next to him, Rupert as representative AOC 11 Group sat on the PMC's left with me alongside. The rest of the top table was filled with distinguished ex-43 officers, including Air Commodore (later ACM Sir Theodore) McEvoy who came closest to me in our association with the two squadrons; he commanded a flight in No 1 squadron in the 1920s, and was squadron commander of No 43 in the 1930s. We took our seats after Padre Hurn had said grace. Percy excelled himself with a five course meal, the wine flowed and there was a hubbub of conversation. When the tables were cleared, decanters of port were placed on the tables, with cigar and cigarette boxes and ashtrays put in strategic positions. The PMC bashed his gavel and Mr Vice proposed the loyal toast, after which the PMC indicated that smoking was permitted. Coffee cups arrived and the stewards filled them up and vanished. Paddy stood guard at the main doors, and no doubt the stewards took it in turn to listen through the key-holes.

In due course, the PMC again bashed his gavel and called on Tom to speak. He kept it short, welcomed the C-in-C and guests, greatly regretted the impending departure of No 43 squadron – which brought forth sardonic responses from all over the place, wished us Godspeed and sat down. The PMC bashed his gavel again for me to speak, and the atmosphere was electric. I didn't keep it short by any means. I gradually raised the tempo with an attack on the decision to move the squadron. This, however you look at it, amounted to ticking off the C-in-

C. From the corner of my eye I noticed that Tom had started to wipe his forehead with a handkerchief, and Rupert kept kicking me on the shin. As I got into my stride, Rupert got up, made his apologies to the PMC and left. I learned later that he went straight back to my house, told my wife that I would be kicked out of the Air Force, and hit the whisky. But Rupert could never stand ugly confrontations.

It would be tedious to give a full account of my speech, not that I made any notes anyway. I was frequently forced to pause until the roars of applause and banging on the table by one-time and serving members of 43 squadron died down. If they were egging me on, there was no need because I was determined to indicate the strength of feeling against the move in any case. I began on a flippant enough note by pulling No 1 squadron's leg. I said they were formed in 1908 as a balloon squadron, and it seemed to me, having watched their pilots landing, they were undecided as to whether they were flying lighter or heavier than air machines. More seriously, No 1 was our sister squadron, although we had the edge on them since we were formed at Tangmere a few months before they were in 1926. I spoke from a position of authority on such matters for I was the only RAF officer ever to have commanded them both. I assured all and sundry that with the removal of No 43 to darkest Scotland, No 1 squadron on its own would not be enough to hold Tangmere together, and it would crumble into the dust sooner than later. Yet the two squadrons had together made Tangmere the crack fighter station in the RAF. A Station is only as good as the squadrons based on it, which the planners at HQFC had signally failed to appreciate. This didn't surprise me because in my view the planners were a bunch of rock apes. (Roars of applause, Tom on the point of a nervous breakdown, Basil Embry glaring into infinity.)

To put it another way, in my view the RAF had not been going long enough to appreciate the true importance of traditional values. Tangmere was a case in point. The Army had learned the importance of the regimental system the hard way. The impending disintegration of Tangmere, which was clearly predictable, was analogous to the Navy scuttling the flagship of the Home Fleet. Perhaps the Staff at HQFC lacked the intellect to assess the true value of the Stations within the Command. Why did they not read and comprehend the various statistics which were sent to them each month? Any moron could, at a glance, see that No 43 produced more flying hours than any other squadron in the Command annually. Its aircraft utilization was way above average. It had registered no flying accidents this year – how did the other squadrons fare in comparison? I knew because I too read the statistics. Perhaps I read them with a clearer eye than the Staff officers who were too busy shovelling around unnecessary bumf to be able to differentiate between their arseholes and their elbows. They gave me a pain in the neck. The proposition that the threat had changed to the nor'easterly approaches might prove to be correct in the fullness of time, but at this stage it was stupid to move No 43 to Leuchars as a counter. Sure, we would clean up ATC procedures and turn Leuchars into a quick-reacting fighter station, but only at the expense of seeing Tangmere decay. The planners had failed to get their priorities right; they usually did.

In any case, Fighter Command was not operational, it was merely an expensive training machine, a spurious panacea to placate the great British public. There was nothing much wrong with the pilots and ground personnel, but the first line aircraft were worth only a hollow laugh. The Meteor was a disastrous waste of money. The much vaunted Hunter, not yet in the front line, was already obsolete. Yet only six years after the war, France was producing supersonic fighters. Why didn't we buy a few squadrons of Mirages, then put the assembly lines onto copying the design? Was national pride more important than the defence of the nation? I finished up by saying that we would go to Leuchars as ordered, but God help Leuchars until it met our operational standards. If the repercussions filtered back to the C-in-C, then let him not blame me, I would just do my job as I saw fit. I sat down to prolonged and noisy applause.

Sir Basil muttered in Tom Prickett's ear and he beckoned to Paddy who was standing impassively by the door. The wine waiters steamed in carrying brandy and liqueur glasses, and dotted bottles round the table while the port went round again. The C-in-C was poured a hefty dose of brandy, and I lit a cigar and waited for the wrath of God to descend. The gavel was bashed and Sir Basil rose to his feet after taking an almost lethal swig of brandy. He began by opening his mouth and shutting it again, but no words came out; his vocal cords were temporarily out of order.

'That's the first time I've ever seen you speechless!' an ex-member of No 43 who'd known Basil for a long time jeered.

Basil glared at him and then found difficulty in modulating his voice. His preference was to scream and yell, but he eventually gained control. It seemed, he said, that the Officer Commanding No 43 squadron thought he knew more about running Fighter Command than he did. I tried to look duly embarrassed with small success. I was enjoying myself; I was on much firmer ground than he was, and I had the majority of the audience behind me. He banged on about the threat from the nor'east and the need to reinforce the area from existing airfields. In this case the Air Ministry had authorized him to take over an existing Coastal Command station, so they obviously believed in the strategic appreciation even if I didn't. Who the hell did

I think I was anyway – Moses? He understood the importance of the two sister squadrons to Tangmere, and he agreed that they had given the place its reputation in the years between the wars. Its importance had been proved beyond doubt as a major Sector station during the war. But times were changing: the important fighting unit was now the squadron, not so much the bricks and mortar of the Station on which it was based. Tangmere wouldn't decay just because one of its squadrons was removed. (How wrong he was!) And if I thought I ran the best squadron in the Command, then let me prove it at Leuchars. But I'd better restrain myself within the bounds of prudence and politesse. If I ran amok like a bull in a china shop, then he would kick me out on my ear.

He sat down to polite applause, and I gave Paddy the nod. Then the fun and games started: The doors were flung open and someone threw Cockie into the room. He flew around squawking, landed with unerring precision on the top table in front of the C-in-C, left some droppings and walked out again. Bagpipes wailed and Dusty Miller marched in wearing kilts, playing a lament. Behind him six bearers dressed in top-hats and black suits carried a coffin draped in the black and white chequered flags of No 43 squadron. The cortège walked slowly round the tables, behind the top table, and out through the doors. Percy then entered in his chef's uniform and tall white hat carrying an evil-smelling haggis on a silver salver and put it on the table in front of the C-in-C. A large card was stuck in, and on it was written in bold script: Presented to AM Sir Basil Embry by No 43 (Fighter) Squadron, Tangmere.

Someone materialized by the grand piano on the platform behind the top table and struck up the opening chords of the squadron song, so familiar to many of the diners. I rose to conduct it as ex-members and serving officers lifted their voices: 'We are the Fighting Forty-three. We come from Sussex by the sea . . .' Dusty Miller returned and marched up and down the room playing deathly laments. When Sir Basil indicated to Tom that he wanted to prepare for leaving, we all stood up as Tom led him off to the cloak-room. Dusty intercepted them as they prepared to leave and played them to the car. Strapped to the roof of the car was the draped coffin which perforce had to accompany Sir Basil to his aircraft.

Epilogue

The next day I despatched the advance party to herald our arrival, to lay claim to our accommodation and to prepare for the arrival of the aircraft. The squadron silver was packed ready to go, and the propeller removed from the wall of the Mess and crated. All personnel packed up their heavy luggage, ends were tied and the final knots tightened. I made a round of farewell visits, and generally inspected the accommodation which had been used. Seventeen aircraft, including the Meteor Mk 7 were taxied to the line in front of the dispersal huts, and the hangar doors were shut and locked. The main party completed the loading, and steamed off in the special train at dawn the next day. In due course the rear party saw us into the air and began to perform the last rites. I made a slow orbit over Bognor allowing the sections to get into close formation. Then I opened my throttles and dived at Tom's flagpole in a final salute. We settled down at 35,000 feet and flew in loose formation on our journey north beyond the Firth of Forth.

It was by no means the end of my visits to Tangmere. When my time with No 43 ran out, Sir Basil Embry magnanimously posted me to his Staff at Bentley Priory. I didn't stay there long and was sent to HQ No 11 Group at nearby Hillingdon as officer in charge of Operations. This brought me in close contact with all the fighter stations in 11 Group, and I flew to them all on Staff visits, including Tangmere. Despite Sir Basil's denial of my prophecies of gloom and doom, it didn't take long for Tangmere to deteriorate into a slum. The writing on the wall had begun before we left when plans had been agreed to build several hundred more married quarters for officers and other ranks. The land selected for this project lay at the top of Job's precious playing fields near the main Chichester to Arundel road. Internal roads were constructed to connect this squalid, red brick housing estate to the minor road leading to the main gates of the Station. It was a marvellous decision even by the lowest Air Ministry standards. Faced with a dwindling population, the housing accommodation was trebled! This also effectively saw the end of the beautifully laid out playing fields, as children ran wild over them. Then No 1 squadron was despatched into the wilderness and turned into a target-towing unit! The RAF's senior squadron was thus given the most ignominious role of them all: from fame to the calm of death for No 1.

All this absurdity was caused by HQFC and the Air Ministry, but the underlying assumption that the threat came from the north-east lay at the root of it. Even granted such an assumption, the elementary facts of a cold war situation were glossed over. The majority of RAF airfields are more or less grouped together in the general area of the north-east Midlands; all the eggs, no matter how addled, are in one basket. A 4 megaton bomb dropped in the middle of the complex would devastate most of them. To reinforce Leuchars with Tangmere-based fighters would take not much more than an hour; and they could be refuelled at Leuchars. If the Soviets made a show of force by sailing a powerful detachment from their fleet through the Dover narrows – perfectly legal on the high seas, no harm would be done by Tangmere-based fighters maintaining cover over the ships, or making low passes, to indicate British disapproval. Tangmere could easily have been retained as *the* show-piece Station in the RAF, for international air displays, as the prize Battle of Britain day airfield, for all sorts of things. It is relatively near to London and lies in the middle of a large holiday catchment area.

There was to be none of that. Fighter Command woke up one morning to find a derelict Station on its hands, so what to do about it? They tried to sell it to the Army for parachute training, but little came of that. Then Signals Command took it over for use as offices until Signals Command passed away from the great lavatory of life. Chichester Council stepped in and laid claim to the empty houses before the walls fell in and turned it all into a council estate. The airfield went under the ploughs. *Ex nihilo nihil fit* in reverse – out of something nothing comes.

And what of the noble ghosts that abounded? What enchanter caused them to flee? But as they used to say before they hit the ground – Fuck 'em all bar the stretcher bearers. May the rock apes be burned alive. It was all so foreseeable.

But the squadrons live and breathe. The demoniac sisters, the terrible twins, have returned to their former glory. No 1 is now equipped with Harrier jump-jets. No 43 will soon discard its Phantoms, so formidable in their time, and re-equip with the latest. Notably, as soon as the RAF could send strike aircraft to the Falklands, they went there together as equal partners. Too much loving care had been put into developing them for it to be otherwise.

Yet a microcosm of Tangmere does exist. When the guys who locate and dig up crashed aircraft first contacted me there were several different groups. They decided to amalgamate and find a place to display their exhibits, and Tangmere seemed to be the obvious venue, so they asked me to become their Patron. I did better than that and persuaded the Duke of Richmond and Gordon to become President, Air Chief Marshal Sir Thomas Prickett to be

Vice President with myself as the other Vice. Surmounting many obstacles and by dint of a tremendous amount of hard work, they finally managed to establish the Tangmere Memorial Museum on the premises. Go and see for yourself. It might give you a taste of old Tangmere, it will certainly not give you a sense of the real glory of the place. I doubt if even this book will achieve that.